A

History of

Penyffordd

and

Penymynydd

bridge
books

Wrexham

A History of Penyffordd and Penymynydd
first published in 2003
by
BRIDGE BOOKS
61 Park Avenue
Wrexham
LL12 7AW

ISBN 1-84494-005-5

A CIP entry for this book is available from the British Library

Printed and bound by
Ashford Colour Press
Gosport, Hampshire

Facing: Ordnance Survey map of Penyffordd and Penymynydd, 1871.

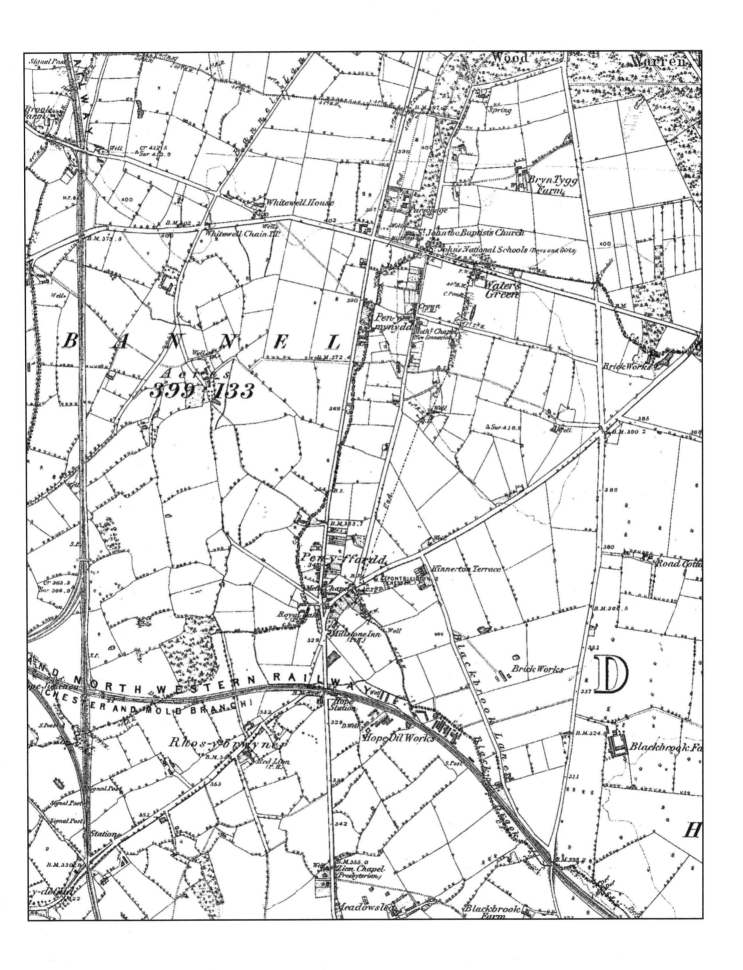

Contents

Foreword

I have always wished that someone would write about the history of Penymynydd and Penyffordd, and now at last Mrs Alison Matthews and Mrs Rhona Phoenix have done just that. We are therefore very grateful to them for carrying out such exhaustive research into our two villages which, before the 1945 post-war building boom, were distinctly separate with a fairly considerable block of land between them.

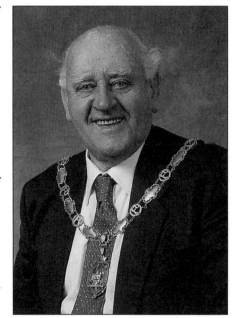

We must recognise the tremendous contribution made by our churches, chapels and Sunday schools. The character and the conduct of the people must have been greatly influenced by attendance at these various places of worship.

For a long period education was provided by Penyffordd Council School and St John the Baptist VP School Penymynydd, and the social life was catered for by three public houses in Penymynydd and three in Penyffordd.

Following the First World War the elders of both villages very wisely decided to build a Memorial Institute in memory of those who had so valiantly given their lives, and this has catered for numerous activities over the years. In more recent times we have seen the establishment of the Royal British Legion Club, which is a further beneficial addition to the amenities of the villages.

We must also record our appreciation of the health care provided by Meadowslea Hospital, first as a sanatorium and more recently as a recuperation hospital for elderly people.

Old and new residents will I am sure enjoy reading this book, and it will be of great benefit to future generations. On behalf of all our residents I wish to thank Alison and Rhona for this valuable creation and I commend it to you.

Councillor Tom Jones, OBE

Acknowledgements

We wish to thank everyone for their kind support and help in writing this brief history.

Mr & Mrs R. Ankers
Mr Phil Arnold
Mr Alec Astbury, MBE
Mrs Beryl Astbury
Mr John Bellis
Mrs G. Birchall
Mrs Faith Bithell
Mrs Gwen Briscoe
Mr L. Byrne
Mrs Sue Cameron
Mrs E. Connah
Mrs Marie Cuckson
Mrs Brenda Davies
Mr Keith Davies
Mr Eric Davies
Mrs Edwina Davies
Mr John Dixon (Saltney Ferry)
Mr & Mrs Terry and Hilary Eccleston
Mr Cyril Edwards
Mr Ivor Edwards
Mrs Joan Edwards
Mrs Kathleen Edwards
Mrs Fox
Mrs D. Graham
Mrs Kathleen Graham
Mrs Glenys Griffiths
Mr John Griffiths

Mr Ron Griffiths
Mrs Ann Harris
Mrs E. Hewitt
Mrs Lilian Hewitt
Mrs June Hibbert
Mrs Sue Hipkiss
Mrs Betty Hughes
Mr A. Jackson
Mrs Gladys Jonathon
Mrs Enfys Jones
Mr Glyn Jones
Mrs Josie Jones
Mr Nigel Jones
Mrs Rose Jones
Mr & Mrs Tecwyn Jones
Mr Tom Jones, OBE
Mr Eric Kelly
Mrs Roberta Kelly
Mr George Leech
Mr Roy Madeley
Mrs Rita Nielson
Mrs G. Nesbitt
Mr & Mrs Price
Mrs Helen Price
Mrs Hazel Shakeshaft
Mr Roy Tunnecliffe
Mrs Jackie Williams

Our special thanks to Mr J. Howell Hughes for loaning us the files of newspaper cuttings his grandfather, J. P. Griffiths, the local reporter for the *Chester Chronicle,* had collected over the years. These have given us a wealth of information about the villages. We are grateful also to Mr Joe Davies who helped us at the beginning of our venture and showed us the layout of the village in the early twentieth century.

We would also like to thank the staff of the Flintshire Record Office at Hawarden for their great help as we struggled to find information; Mr Paul Mason and Miss Elizabeth Pettitt have been extremely patient. It is always a pleasure to visit and work in the Records Office.

Many thanks to Mr Ken Lloyd Gruffydd, MA, for his proof reading, which was invaluable and Mr Reg Carter, the Librarian of the Stephenson Locomotive Society.

Finally, we would like to thank Mr Alister Williams of Bridge Books, for his encouragement and guidance. His professionalism has supported us greatly in this venture.

Introduction

Our aim has been to research the past, in order to show how over the course of time our two villages have developed from the occasional farms, hamlets and wastelands into the villages we know. There have been times when we have included a wider history which does not always appear to relate to our villages, however we believe this to be relevant.

Part One, which we have called 'Setting the Scene', illustrates how much our formation depends on the past. Part Two, 'The Changing Scene', demonstrates the influences which played a part in the growth of our villages. Part Three, is an attempt to recreate the villages of the late nineteenthand twentieth centuries. We also include some crime and mystery.

We have been extremely fortunate talking to many local people about village life and their own experiences. It has been an enjoyable experience and we have had a number of 'Eureka' moments! As the reader will see there are still some mysteries to solve and we do not claim to have covered every aspect of the past, but have tried to produce an accurate portrayal of the history of the villages. Unfortunately for us, neither a Roman soldier nor a Welsh prince dropped their sword or shield. However, it was during the start of our research that we realised how many clues there are which pointed to the distant past.

The area we researched was once sparsely populated, with a number of small hamlets which still exist but which have now become part of the bigger picture. We decided therefore that it would be interesting, before we delved into fuller explanations of the past events, to guide you through the clues that still exist.

We begin with the translation of the village names *i.e.* Penyffordd — top or end of the road and Penymynydd — top or end of the mountain.

One area in Penyffordd which will not be at first obvious, is Rhos y brwyner (Rushman's Moor) through which runs Rhos Road, there are two similarly named farms. This area which covered the Towers estate was first recorded in 1330 as 'Rosbroner'. It is shown on the map and it will be apparent later that it played a significant part in the formation of the village of Penyffordd.

Rhyd y defaid (sheep ford or crossing), lies at this end of Stryt Isa, an ancient road. Stryt Isaf was in 1362 known as le Netherestrete; both versions meaning the lower street.

The Earl of Derby owned considerable amounts of land in the area and there are clues to this in the names of many smallholdings in the area which were called Derby Park. Park Lane was used by railway travellers making their way across the Park at Meadowslea where many sports and games were held.

As you will see by the drawings produced later in the book the old roads and routes were different to the ones used today. Abbot's Lane was known as County Lane and the adjacent fields as County Fields, however on one mid-19th century map it was called the Old Road.

The naming of Wat's Road, Clawdd Offa Farm and Offa's Dyke house is associated with the fact that Wat's Dyke lies to the immediate west of this area and that Offa's Dyke, which is sited further west, was at one time often confused with the earlier Wat's Dyke, hence the house names.

Vounog, a corruption of *Fawnog* (which derives from *mawnog,* meaning a peat bog), is not a recognised spelling, even by the Ordnance Survey. A lease of 'Fownog' [*sic*] tenement was granted by Sir Edward Lloyd of Pengwern, Baronet, to Peter Hughes, yeoman, for twenty-one years 25 December 1770 (or 1778), the nineteenth year of the reign of George III. This appears to cover about 521 acres of land and we believe this is where Meadowslea was built.

It is important to note that references to Hope may mean Penyffordd, as for example, Hope Station, or the fact that Meadowslea was described as being situated in Hope.

You may think of other clues, however we feel that we have given you a taste of how it is possible to trace the past by looking at the present.

We will now begin with the story of how our two villages were formed over the centuries, giving the wider picture to illustrate how major events impacted on our district and utilising the evidence which we have found.

Part One — Setting the Scene

Physical Features

Penyffordd and Penymynydd are situated on a plateau rising above the low lying, and formerly very marshy land alongside the River Dee. The underlying rocks are coal measures and the easy access to good quality coal and clay was the trigger for local industrial development.

Penymynydd is on the higher ground, 137 metres above sea level where Cefn-y-fedw sandstone is very near the surface. This was taken from small quarries for use as building material. Two streams named 'Blackbrook' drain the area and are so called because of the discolouration of the water by the underlying coal deposits. One Blackbrook flows from the Padeswood area, through Rhyd-y-defaid, to join the river Alun near Hope. The second Blackbrook flows under the bridge by the old school to join the Bradbrook stream south-east of the village.

The Distant Past

Flintshire has a long history of human settlement beginning with the Palæolithic culture of the Stone Age (250,000–8,000 BC), when people hunted mammoth and horse and engraved pictures on rocks. There is little recognisable evidence in this area of this period, however we did discover the following description in the *Royal Commission of Ancient Monuments in Wales and Monmouthshire*, published in 1912:

> situated in a field named Erw Garreg Lwyd stretching between Stryt Isa and Wat's Dyke there are two prostrate long stones which may have been formerly Standing Stones. Both are at present being used as steps to hedge stiles. The one at the bottom of the field is made of limestone and measures 4' by 8" by 12" thick. The stone at the top of the field in line with Wat's Dyke is of sandstone and measures 4' by 12" by 9". This last stone is probably Carreg Lwyd (grey stone) after which the field is named.

Megaliths (standing stones) belonged to the Neolithic and Bronze Age, possibly between 3,500 BC and 1,500 BC, and had a number of functions not least serving as the focal point of a community. This was at a time when brown bears, beavers and wild cattle roamed Wales!

The Romans

The Roman conquest of Britain was completed when Wales was finally subdued. This invasion brought about many changes. The fort at Deva (Chester) was built in 70–74 AD at a strategic place for access and control of north Wales and the north-west of England. By the second century this walled town had become an important trading centre for our borderlands. The local British tribe, the Deceangli, after initial strong opposition, appeared to have learned to integrate with the Romans, settling into a peaceful and comfortable life and accepting Roman authority and culture.

The Romans, according to their historian Tacitus, were anxious to conquer Wales because of its valuable lead mines and minerals. One local historian states that it is a possibility that the Romans went through this area in order to reach the lead mines at Halkyn. At this time there would have been a number of settlements in the area comprising a mixture of single farmsteads with fenced or ditched enclosures and small hamlets.

Around 400 AD the Romans began to withdraw from Deva, resulting in more changes as trade and authority began to disappear. Raids from the Picts and Scots from the north and, later, Anglo Saxons from the east, drove the desperate population of the region further west into the mountains and forests leaving a sparsely populated area with much confusion as law and order disintegrated. The so called 'Battle of Chester' in 616 AD resulted in Chester being taken by the Saxons after a great battle between the troops of Aethelfrith, ruler of the Anglian Kingdom of Northumbria, and those of Selyf, Prince of Powys, which resulted in Chester becoming an English stronghold. The Northumbrian armies loomed ominously on the horizon and the Welsh tried desperately to stop Aethelfrith's advance into their territory. Historians regarded this battle as significant because from this time on the British had to continuously defend themselves against various Saxon and, later, Norman invaders resulting in a bitter struggle as they tried to protect their land, livestock, language and traditions. The lands between the rivers Dee and Clwyd became battlegrounds fought over by the armies of Mercia and Northumbria on one side and those of the Gwynedd and Powys on the other. The rise of the kingdom of Mercia posing a real threat in the 7th century.

Wat's Dyke

Wat's Dyke is an ancient linear earthwork, found to the west of Penyffordd, which has existed since at least the early part of the 8th century. It consisted of a bank of earth and a single ditch and is considered to be one of the largest archeological monuments in Britain. It would seem, that the north-eastern part of the present county of

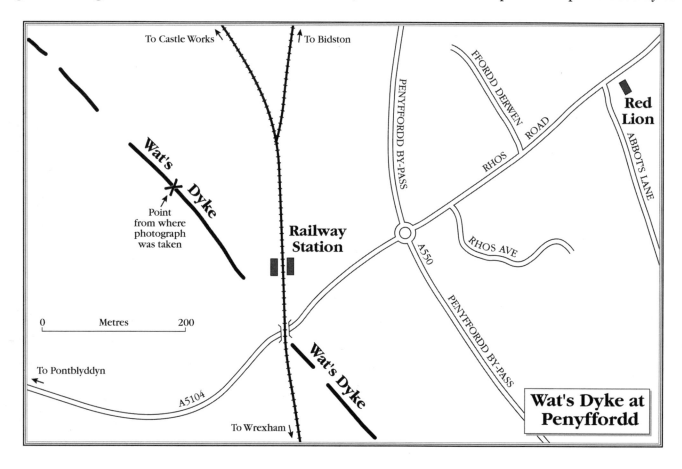

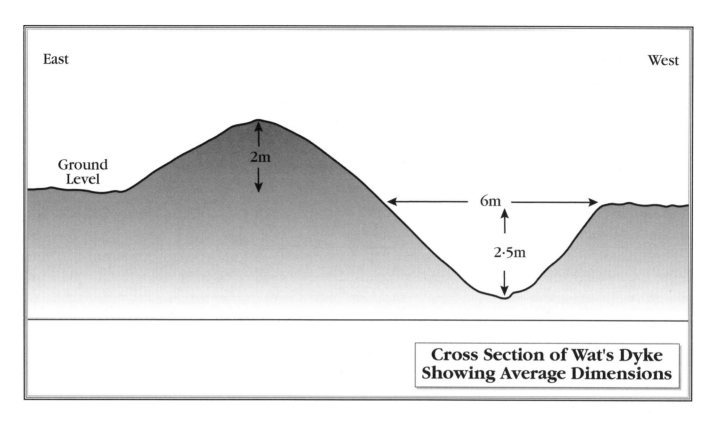

East   West

Ground
Level

2m

6m

2·5m

**Cross Section of Wat's Dyke
Showing Average Dimensions**

Flintshire was permanently under Saxon control although much of the population was British in origin. Wat's Dyke marked the formal boundary and defence dividing Anglo-Saxon Mercia and the Celtic west. The western limit of the region extends for over 62kms from Maesbury in the south to Basingwerk, near Holywell, in the north.

In the parish of Hope, Wat's Dyke often appears to have been confused with Offa's Dyke, which is located further to the west. Historians suggest that this confusion was because in the 1378 charter which was granted to Hope, the 'Offediche' mentioned is really Wat's Dyke.

There is still much speculation about the purpose of Wat's Dyke. A report by the archaeologist Sir Cyril Fox in 1934 described it as a frontier, a boundary rampart, not a line of defence. He believed that it had never been a continuous earthwork but, rather, had only been built where natural features such as rivers, forests and marsh would not serve the same purpose. However, later work on the dyke has led to the theory that pre-historic earthworks along the dyke have, at various times, been re-occupied and re-used thereby suggesting that is was defensive in nature. This linear earthwork consisted of a single ditch and was a form of construction known from when people first became settled farmers, with a need to enclose and defend their land. It is argued that this was

One of the authors showing the height of Wat's Dyke

the first boundary which the Mercians were able to establish between themselves and Welsh. The deep ditch was always on the west (the Welsh) side, which suggests that it was built by the Saxons against the Welsh, not as a defence against a large army but against small groups of raiders whose attacks made agriculture very difficult along the Mercian border. It is also believed to have afforded some protection for Chester.

Now the question is raised, who ordered it to be built and when? Cyril Fox believed that Offa's predecessor Aethelbald (716-57 AD), who ruled the whole of Mercia, was responsible. However it is possible that the dyke could be even earlier *i.e.* late 7th century. Sixty-seven excavations have taken place along the length of Wat's Dyke, the nearest to our area of interest being at Pigeon House Farm (1974) and Clawdd Offa (1978). As research continues radiocarbon dating has suggested an even earlier date, 411-561 AD. This new assessment was based on a find of charcoal at Maes-y-Clawdd near Oswestry. This claim however has been questioned by other historians as it may have nothing to do with the dyke.

Lastly, who was Wat? One suggestion was that the name came from a figure of folklore in the area of Schleswig-Holstein, from which the royal house of Mercia originated. However another historian argues that it could be the name of a local dignitary, or even taken from the saga hero Wada, the Wada Haelsingum, ruler of Haelsingas. We may never know for certain.

By the year 816 AD Mercian power was in decline, as the Saxon kingdom of Wessex became more powerful. It was not until 973 AD, when eight British rulers, amongst them the Prince of Gwynedd and the King of Mercia, submitted to Edgar, ruler of Wessex, and recognised his authority to become King of England.

The territory of north-east Wales (east of the Clwyd estuary) remained disputed and was recaptured by the Welsh, led by Gruffydd ap Llywelyn, ruler of Gwynedd (who was recognised as King of all Wales in 1055). He was also successful in reclaiming lands to the east of Offa's Dyke from English settlers. Although Gruffydd was defeated by Earl Harold Godwinson of Wessex and murdered by Welsh traitors in 1063, his conquest of this area (which had for a time been part of the Norman Earl of Chester's domain) meant that it remained Welsh and later become part of the counties of Flintshire and Denbighshire.

After the death of Gruffydd, Wales was once more broken up into various kingdoms. The campaign had increased the prestige of Earl Harold and marked him out for kingship on the death of King Edward the Confessor in 1066 but, on his accession to the throne of England, he was called upon to defend his claim against William of Normandy.

The Normans, 1066–87

The Norman Conquest is considered to be a crucial turning point in English history. At the time Wales was still largely independent, made up of a loose federation of small princedoms.

In order to understand the predominantly English culture of our area today, it is helpful to have some knowledge of the events which brought this about.

The area was mainly forest, moorland and marsh, and it is understandable why settlement was so difficult. Hamlets, consisting of one or two ploughlands, were by far the most common unit of settlement. The ideal hamlet contained a few homes, closely grouped together and comprised one plough, one kiln for the drying of corn, one chicken, one cat, one cock, one bull and one herdsman who cared for the common herd. Each hamlet was encompassed or adjoined by an open field, beyond which lay common pasture. Examples of such settlements could possibly be on the sites of later hamlets such as Waters Green, Clawdd Offa and Rhyd-y-Defaid.

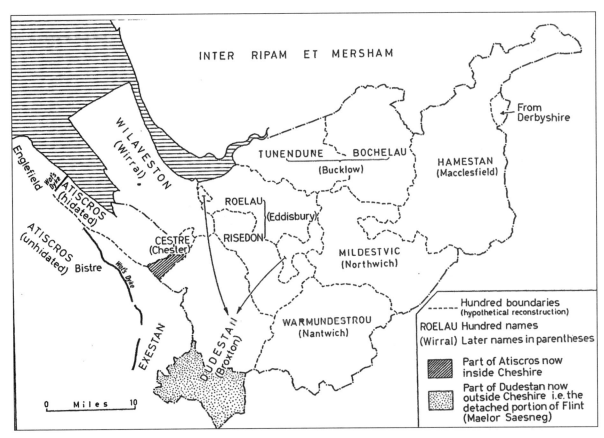

Domesday survey, map showing the Cheshire hundreds.
[Cheshire Community Council Publications Trust]

William the Conqueror was crowned King of England on Christmas day 1066. Chester was still held by Edwin, Earl of Mercia, a Saxon nobleman in 1070, but, before the end of the year and after a brief struggle, Edwin surrendered. At this time William was more concerned with establishing a buffer zone between his kingdom and the Welsh lands to the west than he was with the immediate subjugation of local tribesmen. His policy was one of infiltration rather than conquest, and he appointed his strongest and most formidable trusted associates into what he considered to be vulnerable positions at the head of the natural routeways into Wales *i.e.* Chester Shrewsbury and Hereford. Thus the Norman earls were able to control any route by which an attack might be made against England, not only by the Welsh but also by the Scandinavians, who were settled in Dublin. The earls of Chester, Shrewsbury and Hereford were given virtual independence from the Crown and allowed to rule and conquer lands for themselves, with the help of the lesser Marcher lords (landowners who controlled territory along the March or border land). The great Norman earls were colourful and powerful men with their own army and laws, who were able to enlarge their territories by making war on the Welsh and seizing even more land.

These border, or Marcher lands (of which we are a part), entered into their bloodiest era and suffered large scale devastation, becoming battlegrounds for conflicts between the indigenous Welsh and between the Welsh and the Normans. Because of this there were very few settlements along the borders.

A typical Norman raid would use the art of surprise, attacking and slaughtering the men who tried to flee to the woods, whilst the women were abducted. The manors were wasted by enemy action and, as a result, abandoned.

A Norman knight. [D. Phoenix]

The first of the powerful Marcher lords to take effective control of the area was Hugh of Avranches 1071–1101, the nephew and trusted vassal of the Conqueror, but better known as Hugh the Gross (or Fat) and later as Hugh Lupus (The Wolf). Becoming the first Norman Earl of Chester he was feared and hated, and was described as a coarse worldly man given to gluttony of every kind. He was described by Orderic Vitalis, an English monk of Saint-Evroult in Normandy, who was an historian in this medieval period:

This man, with the help of many cruel barons, shed much Welsh blood. He was not so much lavish as prodigal. His retinue was more like an army than a household, and in giving and receiving he kept no account. Each day he devastated his own land and preferred falconers and huntsmen to cultivators of the same and ministers of heaven. He was so much a slave to gluttony of his belly that weighed down by his fat, he could hardly move. From harlots he had many children of both sexes who almost all came to an unfortunate end.

Orderic went on to describe Earl Hugh's court:

He loved the world and all its pomp which he regarded as the chief part of human happiness. For he was an active soldier, an extravagant giver, and took great pleasure in gaming and debauchery and in jesters, horses and hounds and other vanities. An enormous household which resounded with the noise of a crowd of youths, both noble and common was always in attendance on him.

Hugh pushed rapidly into the front rank of Anglo-Norman society. Inside the earldom of Chester he was all-powerful and, by 1086, succeeded in extending his frontiers to what later became Flintshire and parts of Denbighshire. His cousin Robert played a major role in the Welsh campaign until his death in 1088. Outside his earldom, Hugh had extensive possession in other English counties and a large domain in Normandy. His remarkable record was due to his policy of loyalty to the Crown. Three weeks before his death in July 1101 this far from saintly man turned to the church and became a monk at St Werburgh's in Chester.

King William appointed commissioners to survey his newly acquired territory in 1086. These records became known as the Domesday Book, in which Flintshire and Cheshire are fully described. The land was divided into 'hundreds'. A 'hundred' was a district within a shire, whose assembly of notables and village representatives usually met once a month. These units of land extended from the Dee valley to Wat's Dyke, including the hundreds of Exeston and part of Dudeston and Aticross. The chief manor of Aticross was Hawarden, which consisted of a further eighteen manors. These were comprised of so many hides of land containing large forests *e.g.*: Exeston comprised of twenty-one hides, twenty-one ploughlands, eight plough teams and a population of forty-five persons. Here is an extract from the Domesday Book describing Hope manor in the hundred of Maelor Cymraeg.

Hope — Edwin held it; he was a freeman. 1 hide paying tax. Land for one plough; it is there with 2 villagers. Woodland 2 acres. Value 7s; it was waste and he found it so.

By the end of the Conqueror's reign considerable progress had been made in the subjugation of the native Welsh Princes.

Notes.

A Hide was a unit of land measurement reckoned at 60–120 acres, adequate for one family and its dependents.

A leugu = a measure of length usually a $1^1/_2$ miles = a league.

The people who lived in this area were described as follows;

Villeins = labourers = carried manure, hedge and ditch and other 'humble work'.

Bodor = lived in a small cabin made of mud and wattle and held a small portion of land on condition he supplied eggs, poultry and other articles of food for the table of the lord.

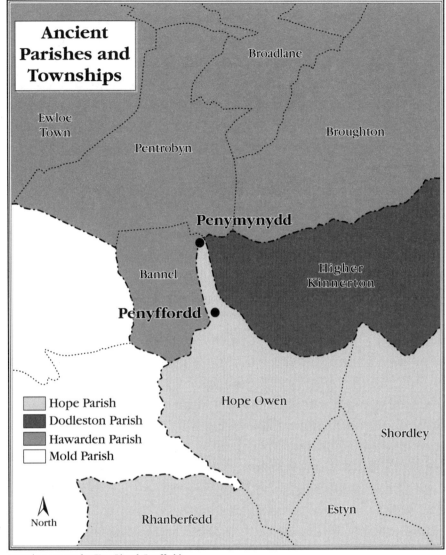

Based on a map by Ken Lloyd Gruffydd

Serfs = lower rank than villeins, reduced to state of bondage.

Waste = more than one meaning, unused land which was deserted because of disease of plough oxen or epidemic, manors "wasted' by enemy action.

The Forest of Hugh which covered an extensive area locally, is described in Domesday.

'of these twenty hides the Earl has all the woodland which he has put in his forest, whence the manors greatly deteriorated. The forest is ten leagues long and three leagues wide. There are four hawks eyries.

The Welsh Princes and Rebellion

The Normans from Chester penetrated into a great deal of north Wales and, although the area colonised was limited, their lordships were established over numerous *cantrefs* and commotes that had previously formed portions of the kingdoms of Gwynedd and Powys. The political situation in the north was, however, reversed during a period of renewed conflict in the reign of William II (1087–1100); after 1093 the Welsh princes of northern Wales gradually recovered from the Normans much of the land that had previously been lost. When Owain Gwynedd died in 1171 he was recognised as a powerful leader holding land from Anglesey to the river Dee. Welsh rule was well established and the area of Hope and Caergwrle were in the possession of the Prince of Powys.

During the early part of the 13th century Llywelyn Fawr, a skilled and highly respected statesman, united all Wales under his leadership bringing peace to the borderlands through his friendship with the Earl of Chester. After his death in 1240 he was succeeded by his son Dafydd who was unable to maintain the unity established by his father and, consequently, lost control of parts of Flintshire. He died suddenly in 1246 and his three nephews, Owain, Llywelyn and Dafydd (the sons of his brother Gruffydd) fought amongst themselves to become ruler of Gwynedd and by 1254, Llywelyn had taken control. The Welsh complained bitterly about the harsh treatment they had received from officials of the Marcher lords and Prince Edward of England (later King Edward I). Llywelyn, with the help of Dafydd, successfully attacked the English forces and drove them out of north Wales and by 1262 was in control of the whole region up to the English border. On 29 September 1267, the Treaty of Montgomery was signed between Gwynedd and England, recognizing Llywelyn as Prince of Wales.

For the next ten years there was an uneasy peace between Llywelyn and England with some of the Welsh lords closest to the border, including Dafydd, aligning themselves with the English king. On the accession of Edward to the throne, Llywelyn refused to pay homage, demanding that Dafydd be surrendered by the English Crown. Eventually, this dispute resulted in the outbreak of war and in 1277 King Edward invaded north Wales and Llywelyn was forced to agree terms which confined his rule to Gwynedd, west of the river Conwy. Dafydd was rewarded by the king and granted land which included the lordship of Hope.

For the next four years Wales was quiet but, gradually, discontent grew over the oppressive rule of the English royal officials in north-west Wales. Many turned to Llywelyn for support but the prince realised the potential outcome and declined to take action. The aggrieved then turned to Dafydd who, in March 1282, damaged his own castle at Caergwrle and attacked Hawarden Castle, slaughtering the English garrison. This overt act of rebellion forced Llywelyn's hand and the prince of Gwynedd took on the leading role in a war against England, the outcome of which was almost a foregone conclusion. Llywelyn was killed in the area around Builth and, a few months later, Dafydd was captured and taken to Shrewsbury where he became the first man to be barbarically executed by being hanged, drawn and quartered.

As a result of the deaths of Llywelyn and Dafydd, Welsh independence came to an end and Edward took control of the territories of the Princes of Gwynedd. He organised the building of a series of castles in north Wales. Chester was the base of this massive undertaking and he conscripted labour from all areas of England.

Edward, determined to subdue the Welsh, proclaimed the Statute of Wales at Rhuddlan on 19 March 1284. The *cantref* of Tegeingl was declared to be the new county of Flint, under the jurisdiction of the King's Justice at Chester and also part of the Earldom of Chester (Edward being the Earl of Chester). The new county was to consist of three separate pieces of land, Tegeingl, Hope and Maelor Saesneg. The English settlers were encouraged to move into the area with generous grants of land set aside by the King in Hopedale.

During the 14th century, however, there were changes in the air. Between 1315 and 1320 the weather became wetter and colder which had a profound effect on agriculture, causing harvest failures as well as livestock epidemics. In June 1349 the 'Black Death' reached Ruthin and spread throughout the area. In England and Wales one third of the population succumbed to this disease, the poorer people, already weakened by harsh living conditions, were especially hard hit. As a result of these disasters there was a drop in the revenue as there were fewer taxpayers, and, as the population moved around to find work not associated to the soil, there developed a glut of untenanted land. This led to tensions within society and a decline in public order.

Between 1360 and 1370 the burgesses in the castellated lands of north Wales demanded a re-issue of Edward I's statutes that Welshmen could only trade in English boroughs. The Hope Charter of February 1399 reveals the full extent of the discrimination which was being forcefully promoted:

> No Welshman can or ought to acquire to himself or his heirs ... any English land for any price, no Burgess was henceforth to be convicted by a Welshman, no Welshman was to hold a market or brew ale within three leagues of the town, all Welshmen of Hopedale were to bring victuals to Hope for sale and Welshmen were prohibited from holding assemblies.

It is little wonder that the Welsh felt angry and discontented. The climate was right for rebellion.

Owain Glyndŵr, a Welsh nobleman, was born *c.* 1354 at Sycharth near Llansilin. In 1400 he made an appeal to the English Crown in an attempt to settle a long-running dispute between himself and Lord Grey of Ruthin. Receiving no satisfaction he carried out a well prepared attack on Ruthin in September and sparked off a major rebellion. In seven days, his troops moving at high speed, he went from Ruthin to Denbigh, Flint, Hawarden, Holt, Oswestry and Welshpool. His main object was to get supplies for a war and he seized food, horses, cattle and weapons. These attacks stirred the nationalistic feelings of the Welsh and during the course of that week hundreds of patriots flocked to join the cause. In 1402, at Pilleth, he destroyed an English army sent against him and captured not only Lord Grey but also Edmund Mortimer, a claimant to the English throne who married his daughter. Glyndŵr was declared Prince of Wales and received ambassadors from both the King of France and the Pope and established itinerant parliaments at Harlech, Machynlleth and Dolgellau.

Henry IV, in order to quell this rebellion, reacted quickly and harshly and in 1401 he passed a series of anti - Welsh legislation. Glyndŵr and his followers undertook guerrilla warfare, which the English found difficult to control and during 1402 he endeavoured to draw the Irish and Scots into the conflict. To counteract this the government passed even further repressive measures. By January 1403 Glyndŵr was posing a more serious threat and infiltrated Flintshire, urging the people to openly revolt. The rebels launched raids in the deep of winter deliberately targeting north-east Wales which had up to now escaped trouble. On 22 February, the town of Hope was burnt — the flames being visible as far away as Chester which, at this time, was the centre of English military power. During the next three years, Glyndŵr was at the height of his power and had little to fear as he moved about Wales.

By 1408 however the tide had turned in England's favour as he was defeated in open battle and returned to guerrilla warfare. The Flintshire Welsh had submitted once more to the King by 1410 and were heavily fined for their part in the rebellion. When Henry V became king in 1413 he twice offered Glyndŵr a pardon, but there was no reponse from the Welsh leader who, like all good legendary figures, disappeared. Was he dead or in hiding? What happened to him is still a mystery.

As both English and Welsh had lived off the land, ransacking farms and towns, the effect of the rebellion had been devastating for Wales. The English parliament imposed a harsh penal system of laws, which remained in force until 1664. Many pardons were granted to Welshmen but others were heavily fined, bringing about their financial ruin.

For the rest of the fifteenth century the country was in economic crisis, made worse by the endemic Black

Death and heavy taxation to pay for a war in France. This was a period of dynastic struggle in England and the War of the Roses commenced in 1455. Wales was regarded as an area from which both sides could draw both money and fighting men. In 1484, after centuries of being part of the Earl of Chester's Welsh estate, Hope Manor was given to Lord Thomas Stanley by Richard III, as a reward for his faithful service to the House of York.

The Act of Union in 1536 brought more changes which affected the border lands as follows:

1. The English system of law was to be applied in Wales and English was to be the language of administration.
2. Land tenure in Wales was to be organised in the same manner as it was in England.
3. The old Marcher lordships were to be abolished and new counties were established in their place.
4. Every shire and county town was to send two representatives to Parliament in London.

It appears that this was a more peaceful time as the County of Flint became stable. Demands grew for corn and timber and the local gentry became better educated, turning their attention to their estates. Conditions in agriculture improved, land was cleared to make way for pasture for the sheep and cattle and various crops including corn became important. As firewood had become scarce there was an increase in the demand for fuel such as coal which was abundant in the area.

The Civil War, 1642–46

In August 1642 King Charles I raised his standard at Nottingham an action which plunged his realm into civil war. Welsh gentry and landowners rallied loyally to the Crown, and paid ship money (a tax levied to build up the King's navy). Wales was important to the Royalist cause, as it was a promising recruiting area, and a gateway to Ireland where even more recruits were to be found. The close proximity of Chester, a Royalist stronghold, meant that the people of north-east Wales were certainly involved in the war. Amongst the troops from Lancashire and Cheshire there were also miners from Flintshire, who were recruited by Roger Mostyn.

The Parliamentarian Commander in Chief was Sir William Brereton, who regarded Wales as '... the magazine where all his majesty's provisions of victualls and men doe proceed'. In 1643, the Parliamentary forces crossed the river Dee after successfully capturing Holt bridge, and the forces, led by Brereton, marched to Wrexham where they stayed the night. The following day he led part of his forces to Hawarden where the castle was surrendered to them by the Royalist occupants. Within two weeks Parliamentarian forces had taken all the Royalist strongholds in Flintshire including Flint, Mold and Holywell. On 18 November, however, around 2,500 Irish and English Royalist troops landed at Mostyn causing the Parliamentarians to retreat to Cheshire. In 1644 Royalists were desperate not to lose ground in North Wales. There was an increase in taxation and a large recruitment drive, which was not very successful. Brereton was desperate to capture Chester but there were constant Royalist challenges.

Although north Wales as a whole was regarded as Royalist territory there were Parliamentarians in the area. In fact Plas Teg, the home of Sir John Trevor, was plundered by Brereton's troops in April 1645. Trevor, however, was a loyal supporter of Parliament and so he submitted a list of articles missing, amongst which were: '1 faire Bible, 1 crossbow, 1 fowling gun, candlesticks and three pounds in money'.

It is highly probable that in this area small cottages, farms and wooded areas were plundered and stripped bare in order to provide for both the Parliamentary and Royalist armies. Soldiers from both sides stole what they could: money, clothes, food, household goods, cattle sheep and horses. Doddleston had a small Parliamentary garrison

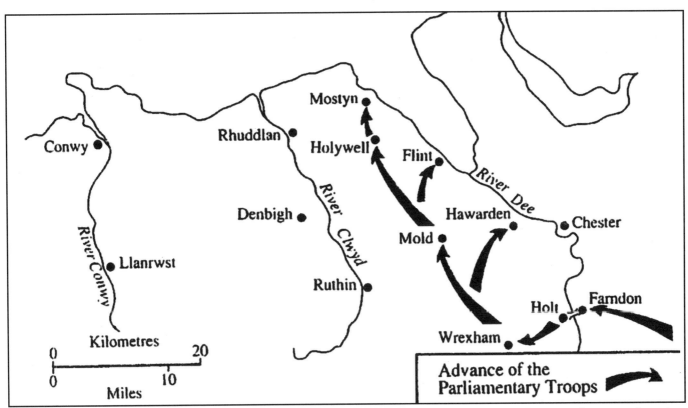

The Parliamentary invasion of north-east Wales, November 1643.
[Cadw: Welsh Historic Monuments. Crown Copyright]

and was a feeding station where stolen cattle and sheep were kept. Between the two armies these borderlands, within a ten mile radius of Chester, were denuded of food. They even went as far as the Berwyn mountains in order to collect sheep and cattle which were driven towards Chester through the vale of Clwyd. Women and children were forced to hide in the countryside and the men, if caught, were made to enlist. In addition, many soldiers were billeted in farms and cottages putting an extra strain on the family to eke out there already meagre resources, churches were ransacked — the lead organ pipes of Wrexham Parish Church were reputedly made into bullets.

In January 1645 Parliamentarian forces again crossed the Dee, marched to Hawarden and seized Holt, and in doing so began to tighten the noose around Chester. Looting and pillaging continued, causing great hardship. On 14 June 1645 the Battle of Naseby was fought near Market Harborough in Leicestershire and King Charles was beaten. On 3 February 1646, Chester, which was desperately short of food, surrendered and Cromwell's forces were then able to move into north Wales. Between 1646 and 1648 the country was still in turmoil and there was much unrest. To make things worse for the poorer people there was a poor harvest in 1647. The Royalists however regrouped and they mounted a new offensive in England and then in Wales 1648.

The result of this war in Flintshire meant that roads and bridges were neglected, local administration was disrupted, churches were desecrated, food was taxed, the countryside was exhausted from the constant search for food, free quarters, fuel and horses and a series of poor harvests forced food prices to rise which meant that ready cash became in short supply.

The Earl of Derby was executed for his part in the Battle of Worcester and the Manor of Hope passed to Sir John Trevor, however it was subsequently restored in 1682. *A compilation entitled Calendar of the Proceedings of the Committee for the Compounding [of Delinquents] 1645–1660,* edited by M. A. E. Green, summarised events which followed:

By the recommendation of Lord President Bradshaw and Sir John Trevor, Roger Hanmer was appointed 23 June 1648 as Steward of the manors of Maylor, Hawarden, Mold and Hope, sequestered from the Earl of Derby ...

10 June 1651 Andrew Ellis of Althrey appt steward of Earl of Derby's estates in the county of Flint ...

The scars of war are quickly healed in a pastoral society and the cattle trade was put on its feet again by the restoration of the English markets and a grant of £3,000 by way of compensation to the drovers by the good office in Parliament of Sir John Glynne of Hawarden.

Part Two: The Changing Scene

The Acts of Enclosure, landlords and the subsequent agricultural developments of Hope Manor, Hawarden and Pentrobin

The Earl of Derby

The structure of land ownership in medieval times meant that the main unit of land division was the manor, held for the Crown in return for specific duties and fealties. By the 18th century rights relating to the commons and wastes were recognised in law as being vested in the lords of the manor and in the freeholders. Settlement in the wastes or encroachment upon the commons needed the consent of the landowner as it infringed on their rights. Even so, because the manorial lords were often remote, as was the case in Hope Manor, squatters could take advantage of this by erecting some kind of shelter for themselves.

The Manor of Hope had 12,000 acres covering the ecclesiastical parishes of Hope, Llanfynydd and Higher Kinnerton, and had the geographical characteristics of a classic borderland manor, a mixture of Welsh culture with English influences.

It first came into the possession of the Stanley family in 1484 when, after centuries of being a part of the Earl of Chester's Welsh estates, it was granted to Lord Thomas Stanley by Richard III '... for singular and faithful service which they have hitherto done us ... not only in favouring our right and title but also repressing the treason and malice of our traitors and rebels who have stirred up perfidious commotions ...' This was a powerful family and the gift of the manor and lordship of Hope, Hopedale, Castle and several estates, was used to buy their loyalty. Not only did they command considerable forces in Cheshire but Stanley had married Margaret Beaufort, the mother of Henry Tudor, Earl of Richmond, who waited in Brittany for a favourable opportunity to make a bid for the throne. That chance came at Bosworth Field in 1485. There the 28 year old Henry Tudor fought King Richard III for the throne. At first it seemed that the king would be victorious until, at the last moment, Lord Stanley's brother Sir William Stanley, threw his support behind their kinsman and tipped the balance in his favour, resulting in the death of Richard III and bringing to an end the War of the Roses. As a result of this the Stanley's acquired still further honours and estates and increased their political influence at court and in the north-west. Their contact with the Manor of Hope however declined. It seems that only once, in the ensuing centuries was there a personal visit by one of the Stanley's (although the fine church at Hope almost certainly benefitted from the patronage of the new king's mother).

The 7th Earl of Derby was executed for his part in the Battle of Worcester 1651, when Charles II was defeated by Cromwell, and it was left to his heir to raise large sums of money to pay fines in order to avoid his property being seized. A rise in rents was one way this could be achieved, however, as one might guess, only a few of the Hope tenants favoured this arrangement, and by 1654 Hope Manor, together with all the other Stanley property held in Flintshire, passed to other owners. Sir John Trevor II (1596–1673) of Trefalun and Plas Teg became the new owner of Hope Manor at a good price and held it until he died. He was a well respected man of considerable standing with the Commonwealth government.

At the Restoration in 1660, the Stanley's, who felt that they had sacrificed much in the interests of the Stuarts, hoped for the return of their property, but Charles II was unwilling to comply with their wishes arguing that Charles, the lately restored 8th Earl of Derby, had freely entered into contracts for the transfer of his former possessions. Earl Charles continued in his efforts by means of a Private Bill but it was not successful. In 1678, the 9th Earl revived the legal battle for the restitution of the Manor of Hope by arguing that Richard III had granted it to the 1st Earl of Derby on condition that it was inherited through the male line only, and so Earl Charles had no right to sell the estate in 1651. As a consequence, by 1682, the Stanley claims to Hope (but not to Hawarden or Mold) had been recognised and the Trevor era was at an end. Edward, the 12th Earl of Derby, on his marriage to Lady Elizabeth Hamilton, only daughter of Duke of Hamilton and Brandon had agreed to try and recover of part of his 'lost' estate in order to provide pin money for his bride. Edward was to become well known as the 'Sporting Earl', founding the two greatest horse flat races, which are still run, the Oaks and the Derby. He had the best studs of racehorses and the best breed of gamecocks in the kingdom. He enjoyed entertaining and gambling for high stakes. The then fashionable sport of cock fighting with his aristocratic friends was the highlight of the first day of the Aintree races. These activities however put considerable strain on his purse strings and so his agents needed to look for new ways in which to raise his income. They would have been well aware of the significance of the numerous Acts of Enclosure being passed throughout the kingdom and of the advantage of replacing small encroachments upon the waste by large well-rented farms. Furthermore, Hope Manor was credited with possessing valuable mineral resources; limestone, lead and coal and these could be extracted by adventurers, who could deal directly with the Earl's agents rather than with a multiplicity of tenancies. The Earl's consent was necessary to implement such a Bill and to pass it through Parliament.

The Hope Act of Enclosure, 1791

As can be seen on the map, Hope Manor consisted of a considerable expanse of land. Rhos-y-brwyner which is at the heart of our modern village of Penyffordd, was one of the commons enclosed. Another large estate was held in the names of Colonel Handfield and Edward Ommaney Wrench, both of Chester. The Colonel was a professional soldier whilst his son-in-law, Wrench, was a successful businessman who also owned the Dee Mills at Handbridge outside Chester. They had bought a number of farms in Uwchymynydd ucha and Penyffordd, as an investment for their families.

At this period of time in Britain, the poor certainly experienced hard times. There were many outside influences which aggravated the lot of the poor, such as the bad harvests of 1780s, also rents had risen steeply. The Seven Years War (1756–1763) in Europe and the American War of Independence (1775–1783), meant a need for more food to feed troops and allies abroad as well as the costs of prosecuting the wars themselves. There was also a considerable rise in population at the end of 18th century. The industrial and agricultural revolution meant that agricultural workers struggled to earn a living as newly invented tools and equipment took the place of these people.

The waste and common lands had been used for grazing cattle, sheep and geese, and as a source of fuel (namely wood and peat), building materials and as a place to catch rabbits for food. The squatters who lived in quickly erected shelters on the common land knew no other way of life and therefore to take away this source of livelihood

Madam,

~~SIR,~~

You are requested to attend a Meeting of the Lords of the Manors of HOPE and DODDLESTON, and Land owners within the two Manors, at Mrs. *Mary Bythell*'s, Inn-keeper in HOPE, on MONDAY the 30th *July* Inftant, at ten o'Clock in the Forenoon, in order to agree upon terms to apply to Parliament for the in-clofing of the Commons and Wafte Lands within the faid Lordfhips, and for afcertaining the Boundaries of the fame.

I am,

Madam,

Your humble Servant,

Jas Wareing

Knowsley
23 July 1787

meant deprivation and starvation for many.

In 1795, 40,000 acres of Flintshire was described as waste or common land. It appears that there were a number of reasons why the Hope Manor area was chosen for enclosure: the community lacked leadership as there was no great landowner present and the population could be described as poor (10% on parish relief) and illiterate. The Earl, with his expensive taste in sport and entertaining, could see an opportunity to gain from a Bill of Enclosure, and so agreed to it being implemented.

The Bill for dividing, allotting and enclosing common and waste grounds within the Manor of Hope in County of Flintshire, was introduced to Parliament in 1791. The process of enclosure had been discussed for some three years without much success but finally progress was being made.

The first task was to survey the manor, which was done by James Heys of Knowsley and Richard Smith of Cheadle, each of them employed by the Derby estate office. Their initial duty after 1 July 1791 was to divide Dodleston Moor by a ditch, leaving 40% in the parish of Doddleston and the remaining 60% in the parish of Hope. This ditch apparently still remains and marks the boundary between England and Wales.

The next stage was the requirement of the commissioners Samuel Weston of Halewood, Richard Hill of Staffordshire, John Thomas of Trefalun, Denbighshire, and Mathew Fletcher of Clifton. Unfortunately John Thomas died and Josiah, the son of Thomas Boydell (the agent for the Trevor and Glynne estates) replaced him. A meeting was convened at the Red Lion, Hope, the home of a Mrs Bithell, on 10 August 1791 at 10a.m. Those with claims to the rights of commons and wastes were to give the commissioners a full true and particular account in writing of such claims, and of 'messuages, lands and hereditments' for which claims were to be made. The petitioners also had to record who was in possession of the land and the acreage involved. All persons neglecting to deliver such claims at the first or second meeting were to be 'excluded and debarred from all rights and titles, claims and interest in the commons or wastes'.

This first meeting was for Hope only, a notice was pinned to the door of Hope Church and three adverts were

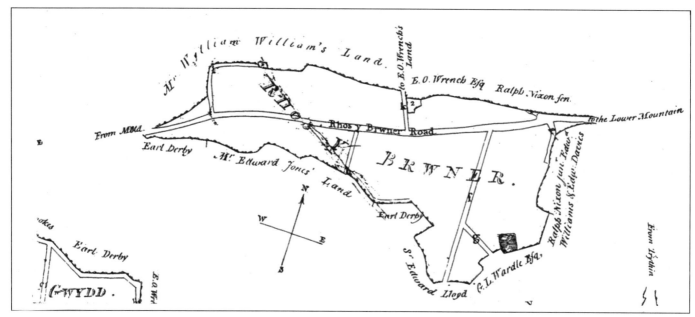

The enclosure plan of the common or waste land at Rhos-y-Brwner in the manor of Hope, 1791.
[FRO QS/DE/7]

inserted in the Chester newspapers.

There were 81 claims in all, which were wide and varied, from Edward O. Wrench to the Mayor and Corporation of Chester which held 239 acres of charity lands (originally devised by Edward I for St John's Hospital without the walls in Chester). Claims were registered by the end of 1791 and the next task was to allocate common and waste land and to plan and construct a system of roads by which each plot could be reached. Surveyors were necessary to continue these public works. To raise funds for this work it was decided to sell off pieces of land, these being auctioned at the Red Lion, Doddleston on 22 June 1792.

The sale bill included the common at Rhos y brwyner (32 acres and 38 perches) which was bought by E. O. Wrench for £530. All the commons that were sold served an adjacent settlement, and as such were an essential element in communal agriculture. In addition three portions of waste were sold, including 10 acres and 20 perches of land adjoining Platt's Farm to John Lloyd for £365, and at a later date 40 acres on Lower Mountain to Richard Barker. Sufficient revenue was raised at the sales to carry out their task of surveying.

In the spring, however, when the stock was turned out to pasture, conflict between local inhabitants and those who had purchased the commons and wastes was inevitable. The initial trouble began with Thomas Jones, a labourer from Uwchmynydd Isa, who was charged on the 12 April 1793 that he did 'wilfully and feloniously pull down a certain fence ... for dividing and inclosing a certain common ... and provided evil example of others in like case.' Eight days later he appeared before two justices to answer for the offence and a warrant of commitment was drawn up and he was conveyed to the county gaol in Flint to await the Great Sessions. On the 20 April his relatives and friends began their efforts to secure his unlawful release from prison. The leaders of this were Richard Roberts, a yeoman of Uwchmynydd Isa, and John Jones, a labourer of Stryt Isa, Thomas' brother. Support for the gaol break was sought all over Flintshire, as far afield as Harwood (Brymbo), Llanfynydd, Shordley and Kinnerton. Early on Monday morning 22 April some 200 men had assembled at Pontblyddin where Richard Roberts was seen giving them ale. Having been regaled in this fashion the crowd moved off on their ten-mile journey to Flint where they arrived at midday. News of their approach had already reached the gaol and so when they arrived it was locked and barred. After much negotiating and violence the prisoner was released and the crowd set off triumphantly. On the return journey, after more refreshment, they decided that the days work had not been completed so they crossed Buckley Mountain to Penyffordd where the recently erected fencing which enclosed Rhos-y-brwyner common was torn down and burnt. Roberts urged his followers to tear it down with the promise that, 'when you get to Caergwrle you shall have meals and drink at Mrs Jones's.' This lady was the owner of the Pigeon House estate but resided in Derby Road, Caergwrle, where her brother managed a tannery. She was at Rhos-y-brwyner with her mother and brother urging men to destroy the work of enclosures. To Peter Jones's son she was reported to have said: 'Why don't you work like the rest? You are a lusty man and how can you be idler than the others? You shall have none of the bread and cheese and ale if you don't work. There are crocks full of ale at Caergwrle.' Before the crowd dispersed further fences were torn down at Rhosygwydd (Goose Green at the top of Platt's Lane) and at the new enclosure adjoining Platt's Farm, Lower Mountain. They stayed the night in Caergwrle ready for the next day's work.

The following morning a hundred or so men began to assemble at Caergwrle at 10a.m., drinking ale before setting out to complete the task of tearing down the fences. News had evidently leaked out as three magistrates arrived. After an hour of fruitless argument the crowd refused to disperse and the Rev. Williams read out the Riot Act. Ignoring this and all threats, the crowd proceeded to wreck fences. By the end of the day all the commons were available for public use once more. The crowd were satisfied, however, this was not the end of the matter as they had underestimated the determination of their opponents who requested that troops be sent to area to assist in restoring order.

At the Great Sessions, which began in Mold on 15 August 1793, before Justice Mills, the trial of those arrested in consequence of the public disorders in Hope was heard. A grand jury was selected from thirty-two prominent landowners in Flintshire and a petty jury from the fifty-two empanelled for the occasion.

Before the court were the prisoners Thomas Jones, Richard Roberts, William Jones, Robert Cook and John Jones. They were found guilty of the charges and would have received hefty sentences. However the Clerk of the Court wrote on the charge sheets the words 'Judgement respited', implying the Judge must have had some doubts about certain aspects of the case. It is apparent that in other areas where there had been disputes the sentences were not harsh. It is clear, as can be seen by the letter, that the gentry did not wish to be too harsh in case this should spark off further unrest. As far as the commissioners were concerned this was an end to the revolt.

The provisions of the Enclosure Act involved considerable public works for the 4,053 acres of which 3,900 were in Hope Manor, about 8½% of which were devoted to roads and byways to allow access to the plots allocated to each claimant. Thus, for the first time, the manor gained an infrastructure of several miles of carriageway, 40 feet wide between their boundaries and, when completed, transferred to the highways in which they were located.

No land was allocated to the poor or for leisure activities but seven plots were set aside in different parts of the manor to be used by the lord and proprietors of estates for purposes of getting stone, gravel, *etc.* for the repair of private roads.

By the 23 October 1797, commissioners had completed the allotment of enclosed lands. From the Earl of Derby's accounts we learn that his tenants took possession in the years 1797–9 which implied that the traditional use of wastes had been suspended for several years while the commons had already been occupied after the fences had been replaced by their new owners. Stonewalling was one method of enclosing *e.g.* the wall near the Red Lion at Penyffordd.

The consequences of the enclosures were mainly noticed in the changes to the land use in the area. In 1794 a

A letter recommending a pardon for the Hope rioters, 1793 [FRO D/LE/687].

report of the production of corn in Hope Parish and township of Kinnerton read:

... the average produce of wheat per acre in this parish is about 13 bushels, ...barley 15 bushels per acre, ... oats 20 bushels per acre ... in Hope Owen acres of wheat = 50, barley = 60, oats =70. Total wheat = 5056, barley 7002, oats 9760.

Enclosure in Penymynydd

The Glynne family of Hawarden

In 1653 Charles, the 8th Earl of Derby sold the Lordship of Hawarden to Sir John Glynne of Glynllifon of Caernarfonshire for £1,700.

When Sir John Glynne (1712-77), 6th Baronet, inherited the estate he came to live at Broad Lane Hall in 1723. He married Honora Conway of Bodrhyddan, Flintshire. She inherited Ravenscroft lands in the area and so the Glynne's became major landowners in Hawarden, Hope, Kinnerton and Doddleston. Sir John Glynne took a great interest in the management and development of his estates. When he died in 1777 he was succeeded in 1780 by his newly born grandson, Sir Stephen Richard Glynne, whose mother, Mary, a shrewd business woman, ensured that the estate continued to prosper until he was of age.

In 1798 there was a proposal for the dividing, allotting and enclosing of all commons and waste lands in townships of Broughton, Pentrobin and Bannel within the Manor and Parish of Hawarden in the County of Flint, this document also included Penymynydd. Altogether about 600 acres were involved. Sir Stephen Richard Glynne, Baronet and Lord of the Manor of Hawarden was entitled to the soil of the commons and waste lands and to the royalties. There was also a large rabbit warren upon a certain part and wastelands in the town of Broughton to which he held the rights. Josiah Boydell and Joseph Potts were appointed to act as as Commissioners and notices were posted on the south door of the Hawarden Parish Church and also in the Chester newspapers and the first meeting was held at the 'house of Lydia Howell at the sign of The Fox' in Hawarden on Tuesday 8 May 1798 (the second meeting was on 7 June 1798 and the third on 16 July 1798). This Act of Enclosure finally went through in November 1802.

There does not appear to have been any disruption in the Penymynydd area as there was in Penyffordd. Perhaps this was because there was a resident landlord, namely Sir Stephen R. Glynne. Sir Stephen died suddenly in 1815 leaving a widow and four young children. His eldest son Stephen inherited the title at the age of eight years. He never married but his sister Catherine married William Ewart Gladstone, the future prime minister, in 1839. Sir Stephen Glynne had no interest in the estate and due to a badly managed industrial venture in Staffordshire his finances were in a desperate state. To help, Gladstone brought his family to live in Hawarden Castle and also paid off most of Sir Stephen's large debt. Through legal and financial arrangements Sir Stephen ensured that Gladstone's eldest son Willy would inherit the estate on the deaths of Stephen and his two brothers, and so the estate eventually transferred to the Gladstone family.

Agriculture

The following accounts may give you some idea of agricultural development in our area in the eighteenth and nineteenth centuries.

Agriculture had been the largest single employer of labour throughout the eighteenth century, even as late as 1811 one third of the labour force was employed in agriculture, forestry and fishing. However the lot of most rural labourers deteriorated from the 1780s until at least the 1850s. From 1770 to 1813 the price of foodstuffs had risen, alongside unemployment, with an increase in available labour. Some historians argue that enclosures brought about more work as there was a need to bring the commons under the plough and increase the nation's foodstock, on the other hand others blamed it for rural pauperisation as many went to find work in the towns and cities.

Documents from the Leeswood estate detail the cost of articles, livestock and labour in the area in 1787:

Labour	*Livestock/goods*
Cowmen 10s. 6d.	30 tons limestone at 2s. 6d. a ton = £3 15s.
Fencing 12s. 0d.	candles and oil 2s. 6d.
Labourer 12s. 0d.	200 Quicksets at 6d. each
Labour 5 days ditching 17s. 0d.	clover seed 2s. 9d. per bag
The mole catcher 1/2 year allowance 10s. 6d.	Cow £5 0s.
2 months wages £2 10s. labourer	Land Tax £2 11s. 8d.
2 teams 5 days ploughing at 5s. each £2. 10s.	Iron for ploughs £5 2s. 2d. wear + tear
Cowmen 10s. 6d.	
2 oxen bought at Ruthin fair £13 16s. 0d. by John Lewis who had 3s. 0d. for buying them.	
Team of horses man + boy 4s. 6d.	Black heifer bought at Mold fair £4 10s.
3 men, 3 days carrying kilns out, 12s. each, £9	Sheep x £9 10s. 6d. each
Moving + gathering, carrying 2s. 6d.	Tythe hay £4 10s. 0d.

In the year 1818 the Flintshire Agricultural Society had devised rules and orders to encourage both agriculture and industry. Their inaugural meeting was held at the Leeswood Arms Mold, where Sir Thomas Mostyn, Bart,. M.P., was elected President.

A report on the state of agriculture on the Hawarden estate 1843 stated:

The Bannel is cold and wet but with strong improvable soil ... around Hope some good grass and turnip soil but rest poor, wet, cold, soil lying on retentive subsoil. Abundance of dung and other descriptions can be had from Chester at a very moderate price. Many of the lanes and farm roads are in a most indifferent state of repair. A considerable portion of land was in the hands of smaller classes of occupier who appear to neglect the cultivation of acres and to find employment carrying coal to Chester or in working mines or public works.

Cattle on the estate were of mixed breed, a cross between Ayrshire, Hereford and a local breed, being raised for dairy purposes. Cattle were sent to the Smithfield market Liverpool. Sheep had also been introduced. The crops which were rotated at this time possibly on a seven-year rotation period. On a farm of 300 acres it was split as follows:

> 30 acres in potatoes, beans and turnip drilled
>
> 30 acres wheat drilled
>
> 30 acres barley with 8lbs of red clover, 4lbs of white clover, 2 of yellow plus 1½ lbs (clover enabled nitrogen to be put back into the soil) bushels of stickney or paceys rye grass seed per acre
>
> 30 acre clover, hay one cut only
>
> 30 acre pasture
>
> 30 acre oats or wheat
>
> 30 acre meadow top dresses and mowed the remaining 90 acre pasture.
>
> Carrots were also mentioned
>
> On this estate there was game fishing and shooting.

According to this document there were forty-six cottages in Penymynydd, and the Penymynydd Inn, (White Lion) lay beside the turnpike road to Buckley.

Small-holdings and allotments

It was in 1908 that the Small Holdings and Allotments Act was passed. The definition of an allotment extended to five acres and a smallholding from one acre to fifty acres. This Act followed many others, which had tried to improve land use. Mr J. P. Griffiths was appointed in 1909 as a Special Officer for Flintshire. He assessed the number of applicants and quantity of land required, especially in Hawarden, Queensferry, Buckley, Penyffordd, Broughton, Bretton and Saltney. The compulsory purchase of land from landowners was controversial, however, this land was sold on easy terms to ex-sailors, warrant and petty officers and non-commissioned class, fire brigade, civil servants, ex-policemen and others who have honourable public or private service. It was felt that there was a need for this class of resident in our country villages. The belief being that they would be useful as scout masters, organisers of clubs and sports. These smallholdings were certainly an asset during time of war because of intense cultivation of crops etc. Milk production was said to be the backbone of the farming industry in Flintshire.

In our area there were a few smallholdings, many of which were named Derby Park. One, which is on the Wrexham Road and is now known as Paddock Farm, consisted of fourteen acres. This land was rotated to grow barley, corn, and grass for cattle grazing.

Poor Law

Pre industrial Britain had a social policy based on the Elizabethan Poor Law and the 1662 Act of Settlement, which prescribed the state's duties for the maintenance of the old, the sick and the poor. This was the traditional core of social policy. The Poor Law report on which the Act of 1834 was based, suggested that the price of labour should rise when labour was scarce and fall when plentiful. If men were out of work it was considered to be a moral failing, to be corrected by indoor relief in a union workhouse.

The horses 'Gypsy' and 'Flower' turning the hay, 1930.

It was not until the last quarter of the century that a more humane approach was put in place. Poor relief was a major item in the expenditure of most parishes and, by the late eighteenth century, was growing at an alarming rate. It frequently extended to regular outdoor relief while orphans and those unable to work went into the workhouses, hence indoor relief. Therefore, in order to help the poor, rates became a compulsory levy on property owners in each parish. For example, particulars of assessment and collection of the poor rate of Hope parish is illustrated in an old Rate Book of 1883/84. Notices giving the rate of £1 6s. in the pound, were posted on Church and Chapel doors. The following entries are just a portion of those having to pay this poor rate,

Wilcock and Co. owners of the Hope Oil works £2 8s. 8d.

Blackbrook William Higgins £2 9s. 4d.

F. A. Frost Meadowslea and plantations £4 3s. 10d.

Millstone George Hollins Wilderspool brewery and land £1 16s. 5d. plus 12s. 2d.

The Crown Thomas Griffiths occupier £1 0s. 3d.

There were those who were in receipt of outdoor relief October 1897:

Penymynydd x 4 , Penyffordd x 11, most receiving between 2s. 6d. and 3s. 0d.

The number of houses in this area at this time were:

Stryt Isa — 10, Penyffordd — 59 plus inns and school, Penymynydd — 41 plus inns and school, Bradbrook — 3, Blackbrook — 3, Lower Mountain — 8, Smithy — 3.

Industry

The enclosure of land, which went on relentlessly in the eighteenth century, was initially labour intensive. However, other workers were engaged in local industrial activities. Stone was quarried for building material, coal extracted from small pits for domestic fuel and lime burning. There were also homecraft workers such as weavers, wheelwrights, joiners, shoemakers, tailors and blacksmiths. In the Buckley area there were brickworks and potteries producing domestic earthenware.

From about 1750 great economic changes took place. New roads, canals (and later railways) were built. The river Dee had already been canalised between Chester and Flint (1737) allowing shipping easy access to the ports along the Dee.

As the Industrial Revolution took hold so the demand grew for bricks of all types. The Buckley potters such as Jonathan Catherall altered their kilns and adapted their machinery to increase production to meet this demand. Tramways were constructed to take bricks and earthenware pottery down to the docks on the Dee for shipment around Britain and Ireland. The number of brickworks and potteries steadily increased and by 1780 there were fourteen separate establishments in the district.

On the Ordnance Survey map of 1871, there are two brickworks near Penyffordd, one along Terrace Lane, and the second, larger, works with three kilns on the Penyffordd – Chester road, just before the junction with the A5104. One resident recalls his grandfather describing a clay pit opposite the old school, where slop or common bricks were made, which were not the same quality as the Buckley bricks.

Inevitably there was a great demand for coal to fuel both old and new industries in the area, and many new pits were sunk around Buckley. For many families, especially those in Penymynydd, coalmining became full time employment. In the 1861 census there were 10 miners but by the 1891 census 38 men were employed in the mines close to Penymynydd.

In the first half of the nineteenth century child labour was invaluable, as children were an essential part of the industrial process. In fact adult workers depended very heavily on children to help them, as the child's money was often essential for family survival. An average wage for a general labourer was £1 a week. In 1841 a boy working in agriculture earned 2s. a week, if he worked in coal mining he could earn 2s. per day.

Here are some sample prices in north Wales in 1838, which gives us an idea of the cost of living;

> White loaf 3d.
>
> Brown loaf 2¹/2d.
>
> Candles (lb) 7d.
>
> Tea (lb)   5s.
>
> Coal (ton)   8s.
>
> Pint of ale   1¹/2d.
>
> Butchers meat 4¹/2d. to 6¹/2d.

The 1841 Commission on Children's Employment shows that miners families lived mostly on bread, butter, potatoes, milk or broth, sometimes bacon, but very little meat except on Sundays. Poor living conditions, hunger, disease and long hours of work meant a hard life for the family.

In 1850 in Scotland, James Young patented a process for distilling oil from certain types of coal. About 1860 it was found that cannel coal and oil shale deposits lying beneath Leeswood, Padeswood and Nercwys could be distilled for oil making. Mineral Statistics Report of 1865 gave the yield as follows:

> Curly cannel coal produced 80 gallons of crude oil per ton
> Smooth cannel coal produced 35 gallons of crude oil per ton
> Shale cannel coal produced 33 gallons of crude oil per ton

The crude oil was further refined to make the following products, burning oil, lubricating oil, liquid grease and stiff grease. Many oil works were set up in the area, three were established near the railway station in the centre of Penyffordd. Cannel coal and shale were brought to the works by rail from local mines at Padeswood, Coed Talon and Leeswood, and then processed in cast iron retorts at 800°F. The Mineral Statistic Report of 1865 detailed the three oil works in Penyffordd: Roger Jones and Company. E. G. Buttery and Company (taken over later by Peter Wilcock) and The Cambrian Oil Company

The boom years for oil distillation from coal were between 1860 and 1880. It was the development of the American oil fields, which led to a rapid decline in the home industry, as imported American oil could be sold much more cheaply.

Wilcock and Piercy at the Royal Cambrian Works in Penyffordd continued to manufacture all kinds of oils and grease for collieries, iron works and other local industries until around 1900. Older residents recall being told of paraffin being bought direct from the works for lamps to light homes. It was also delivered around the villages and outlying districts by horse and cart. The oil works provided employment for nine local men when the census was taken in 1871. One worker lost his sense of smell and died of cancer, possibly as a result of poor working conditions. The oil works must have been a source of pollution as the gases were released into the atmosphere and were certainly unpleasant. The police also checked Blackbrook for signs of pollution from the oil works. Today there is no trace of the oil works except for the house 'Rosewood' which has been converted from the offices of the business.

A close study of the census returns from 1861 and 1901 for Penyffordd and Penymynydd

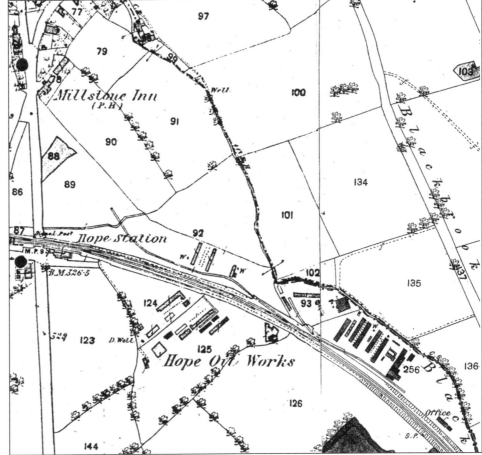

1871 OS map (25" to 1 mile), showing the oil works in Penyffordd. [FRO]

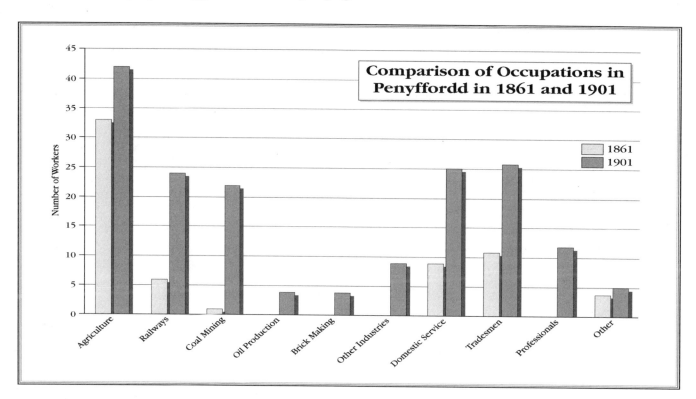

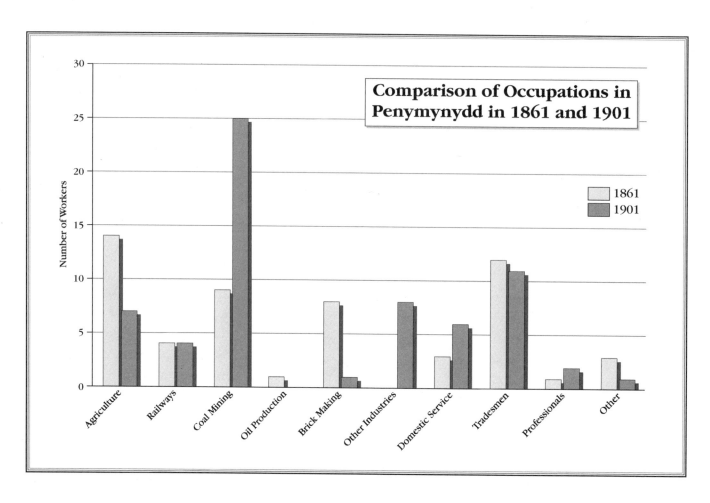

reflects the growth in industrial activity. In Pen-ymynydd in 1861, agricultural work was still the main liveli-hood with some coal mining and brickmaking, how-ever by 1901 coal mining was the chief occupation for males. For females the numbers involved in domestic work remained constant over the 40 years.

In Penyffordd, the 1901 census statistics show an increase in population. Agri-culture still remained the major occupation but there were more coal miners, domestic workers, tradesmen and shopkeepers. The two railways running through the village provided work for 24 men amongst them 2 station masters, 3 porters, 6 signal men, 2 shunters, 3 yardmen and 3 platelayers. During the next 100 years employment patterns reflected the decline of the old industries of coal mining, brickmaking and pottery manufacture, with the rise of other industries.

With revolutionised technology industry continued to expand, John Summers set up a steel plant at Shotton in 1896 which grew into a huge works employing, at its peak, 13,000 people. The coal mines at Llay Main and Gresford were also large providers of work. Vickers Armstrong (later de Havillands) the aircraft factory in Broughton which started in 1937 also had a large workforce. During the Second World War many women worked in industries such as the aircraft factory, learning the men's jobs *i.e.* welding, replacing the men on active service.

After the war cement was in great demand for rebuilding schemes. In 1949 F. L. Smith opened a cement works by Padeswood Hall, formerly a horticultural college. In 1966 the plant was extended and the annual cement production increased to 500,000 tonnes. In 1982 Castle acquired the company from Tunnel Cement. Throughout the years the works have provided employment both directly and indirectly for many local people.

In the present century men and women work in various capacities from the service industries to manufacturing and electronics, commuting many miles via the transport of this age. A far cry from the toil in the fields and housework.

Transport

Footpaths–Modern Transport

Before the railway age, trackways, footpaths and roads provided the principal means of overland communication. As can be seen by the sketch map, we would suggest these were the main routes in our area.

It was however costly and difficult to maintain these links with other villages and towns. The Highway Act of 1555 remained in force for 280 years and specified that persons holding land, arable or pasture, with an annual value of £50 or more had to supply two men with oxen, a cart and tools to repair the highways for four consecutive days each year, this was increased to six days in 1563.

From medieval times until the eighteenth century the inhabitants of each village were expected to contribute towards the work and expense involved in maintaining and repairing roads which passed through their village. Common Law and various authorities enforced these duties, each with a differing amount of success.

Until Tudor times, in the sixteenth century, these local organisers were the medieval co-operate units — the church, the manorial court, the guilds and the borough co-operations. From these very early times the history of road maintenance appears to have been less than satisfactory, with a record of half-hearted and unskilled efforts. Complaints by travellers of the disrepair and neglect, which made travel slow and hazardous, were numerous. The Tudor government endeavoured to attempt to reorganise the Act of 1555, making provision for each parish to administer and regularise the methods of highway maintenance and authorised the appointment of parish

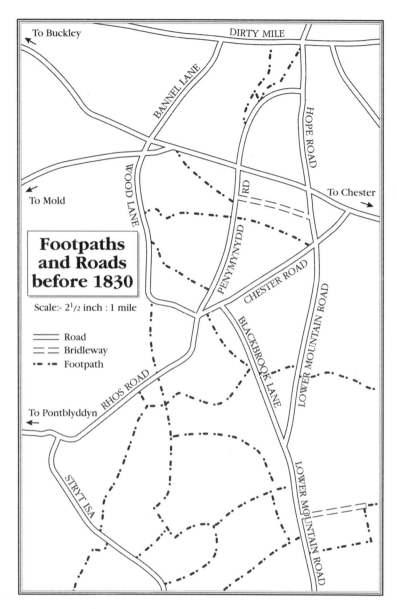

Footpaths and Roads before 1830

Scale:- 2½ inch : 1 mile

═══ Road
═ ═ Bridleway
•─ •─ Footpath

surveyors, who were the descendants of the medieval 'way wardens'.

Statute labour supervised at the Quarter Sessions was an aspect of the work of a justice of the peace. From the end of the seventeenth century a parish rate was levied to provide hired labour in place of unpaid labour.

In 1632, the number of coal pits in this area caused problems for travellers. One report stated:

... there is a waine leadinge from Knowle Hill to Estyn (Hope) and from there to Wrexham full of ould colepitts. ... uncrowne, some not fillt up and that ... there are within the Townships of Bannel and Pentrehobin and bene dangerous for travellers and passingers when passeth that waye ...'

The first Turnpike Act was introduced in 1663 and was followed by many others into the eighteenth century. In order to take charge of the whole road system, the formation of the local Turnpike Trust in 1752 was seen as a solution with the power to levy tolls, which could be spent on making the roads tolerable. By 1800 north Wales had 1,000 miles of turnpike roads.

In spite of these provisions roads in the mid-eighteenth century were still dreadful, with deep ruts and uneven surfaces, in fact a Welsh journey became synonymous with a very uncomfortable ride! In the Quarter Session Minute Book for 17 January 1788 the inhabitants of Hope Owen (one of the townships of the parish of Hope) were fined £25 for not repairing the highway along Stryt Isa.

By 1794 the turnpike roads were kept in better repair in general but cross and parochial roads were in a wretched state. They were so bad that in many places in winter it was difficult and dangerous to travel on horseback and virtually impossible to get a carriage to pass along them. They were uncommonly narrow and low, often answering the double purpose of both road and drain. In 1821 the cost of road widening from Pontblyddyn to Penyffordd was £647 including the purchase of land.

In 1834 a new road was proposed from Abermorddu to the Lower King's Ferry which went through our village. Mr. James Boydell of Hawarden was the surveyor and land had to be bought, in order to construct the road, from the biggest landowner Lord Derby. This road is now the Wrexham Road–Vounog Hill–Hawarden Road.

The turnpike revenues made it possible to employ expert professional surveyors and road engineers. Macadam became the new road surfacing material in the nineteenth century.

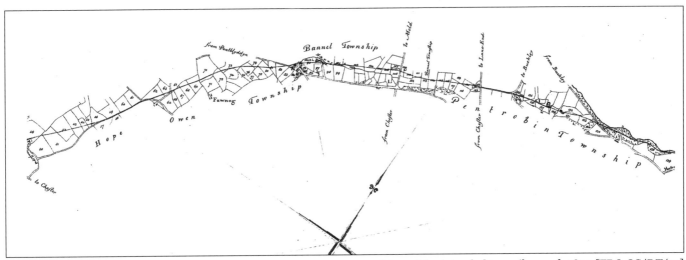

Plan of the intended turnpike road, 1834 [FRO QS/DT/15]

The following example gives us an idea of the costs involved when travelling. This is an extract from the Lower King's Ferry, Turnpike Act and Abermorddu branch:

For every horse, mule or other beast drawing a coach, chariot, phaeton, colash, curricle, chaise, diligence, caravan, hearse or litter — 9 pence.

For every horse mule or beast drawing a waggon, wain cart or such like carriage — 10pence.

For every horse unladen — 2pence.

For every ass drawing any sort of carriage — 6 pence.

For every ass not drawing — 1penny.

For every drove of oxen, cows, or other neat cattle — 1 shilling and 8 pence per score and so in proportion for any greater or lesser number.

For every drove of calves, hogs, sheep or lambs — 10pence per score and so in proportion for greater or lesser number.

For every horse etc. drawing in waggons or carts having fellies of the wheels thereof of the breadth of 6 inches or upwards at the bottom of the soles thereof — 6 pence — less than 6 inches and not less than $4^1/_2$ inches — 9 pence, less than $4^1/_2$ inches — 1 shilling.

For every carriage propelled or set or kept in motion by steam or machinery or by any other agency than animal power — 1 shilling for each wheel thereof.

And for every waggon wain coat or such like carriage passing upon any of the sand roads comprising in this act having nails on the tire of the wheels thereof projecting more than $1/_4$ inch above such tire — 10 shillings.

There were many toll bars, chains and houses situated in our area, these are a few that we were able to identify: Tinkersdale, Dobshill chain, Whitewell toll house (Bannel),

The crossroads, Penymynydd.

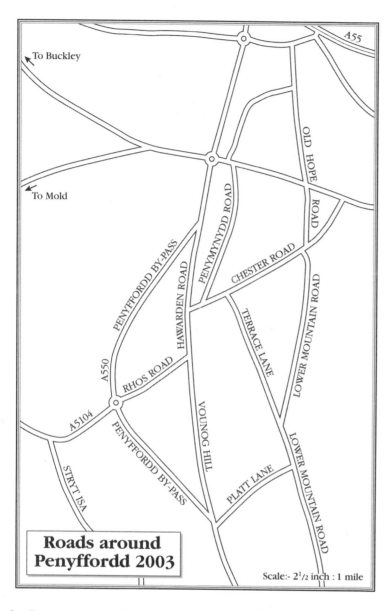

Roads around Penyffordd 2003

Scale:- 2½ inch : 1 mile

Hawarden Road just below the Penymynydd roundabout, a toll house on the way to Pontblyddyn which still stands, and one almost opposite Pigeon House Lane Hope.

Gradually a long distance overland road system evolved, linking together regional centres and providing a network of inter-connected routes. From the mid-nineteenth century, as turnpike roads extended throughout much of southern England, north into Scotland and west into Wales, it was possible to see the beginnings of a fully fledged transport system. These routes focused on certain centres, such as market towns, and confirmed the evolving relationships between emergent towns and the countryside within the various regions. The turnpike roads acted as means of town and country integration. However problems of the cost of tithes became apparent in some areas mostly south Wales, with the advent of Rebecca.

The basic idea of local inhabitants' responsibility organised by parochial officials remained in force until the late nineteenth century, when the Local Government Act of 1894 finally removed all remaining parish authority to the new district councils.

The layout of our roads remained the same for 150 years. The Penymynydd roundabout was built 1960–1 to replace the crossroads, which were dangerous. The Penyffordd by-pass was officially opened on 21 May 1987, relieving the village of traffic congestion, pollution and noise.

The Drovers

The drovers of the eighteenth and nineteenth centuries unwittingly played a vital part in the forging of an economic and cultural link between England and Wales, which was beneficial to both countries. The Corwen road which crosses Blackbrook just past the end of Stryt Isa and opposite Rhyd y defaid (which incidentally means sheep ford or crossing), was such a drover's route. In fact two drovers, Robert Hough and son were living in Penyffordd in 1851.

Cattle and sheep were taken from as far as Bala to the markets of Chester, Mold and Wrexham, even as far as Smithfield in Liverpool. Drovers received cattle on trust, paying the farmer on the way back from the market. Travellers would often find their path blocked by herds of cattle and sheep on their way to the markets. The noise of these herded animals could be heard from far away, and so the local farmers had to lock up their own animals for fear they may be taken with the herds. An unscrupulous drover, however, could bring disaster to the trusting small holder, who most of the time lived just above the poverty line.

The drovers were mainly described as a formidable lot with a lack of grace. Twm o'r Nant, who regarded them as charlatans, records one such bardic rebuke:

> The old drover sleeps, his term completed
> throughout his wasted life he cheated
> his world is now a narrow bed
> Fie! Let him cheat her instead

In the autumn of 1865 the deadly cattle plague, rinderpest or contagious typhus, broke out. It was lethal as veterinary skills were basic and the agricultural industry was ill-prepared to deal with the situation. Even so, amazingly, droving was allowed to continue. This was the interim period before railway transport made 'droving' obsolete.

Railways

The development of major through routes by the railway companies in the nineteenth century, as well as those by road, would bring great changes to travel and communication throughout the British Isles. It was this rapid development following the period of high speculative investment during the 1840s — the so-called railway mania — which was largely responsible for the transport revolution between 1840 and 1852.

Railways transformed the face of Britain, particularly in villages such as ours. Not only did they revolutionise the travel habits of the people, enabling them to travel further, but they also had an enormous effect on industry, as goods could be transported more cheaply. Within a period of 20 years a virtually countrywide railway network of some 7,000 miles had been laid — about a third of which had been built in the period 1846–50.

Whilst railways replaced the longer distance road carrier services, there was still a need for the local carriers, using a horse and carriage or cart, who continued to exist in most districts, carrying goods and passengers from the local rail head to the villages, hamlets, farms and industries. These remained vital links between market town and countryside.

With this more convenient way of travelling however, migration to north-east Wales was much easier. Indeed, it is possible to see in the 1861 census the number of people who came into our area just to work on the railways.

In Penyffordd, temporary housing was provided for some railway workers in Terrace Lane. These cottages were

The view along the platform at Hope & Penyffordd Station, 1957. A Fowler 2-6-2T engine (40060) leaves for Chester. [W. A. Camwell, The Stephenson Locomotive Society]

Above: Beryl Hewitt, Pam Hewitt and Susan Garston admiring the garden at Hope & Penyffordd station in 1955.

Above: The last passenger train about to leave Penyffordd in 1963. On the platform are: Miss Nellie Hughes, Mr Fred Foster, Mrs Brenda Davies and Mrs Alice Williams.

Above: The view along Vounog Hill, towards the level crossing at Hope & Penyffordd station, c. 1910.

Above: Hope & Penyffordd station, c.1927.

Right: Hope & Penyffordd station.

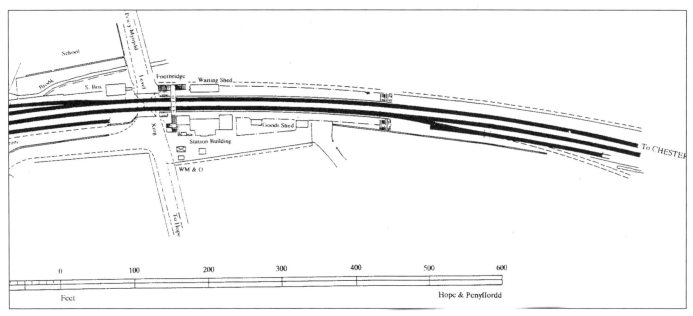

Plan of Hope & Penyffordd Station [Gregory K. Fox]

known as Kinnerton Terrace (in the Parish of Dodleston at this time) hence the name Terrace Lane. They were demolished when no longer needed. Many of the labourers who worked, built and travelled on the new railway were from as far away as Ireland.

In the 1861 census there are many railway labourers mentioned, these are just an example:

Penyffordd

George Millington Railway labourer born Cheshire, Whitby

Thomas Elliot Railway labourer born Ireland, Dublin

The Hope and Penyffordd Railway Stationmaster was John Hasling from Preston in Lancashire.

Penymynydd

William Beaven Railway labourer born Flintshire, Hawarden

John Griffiths Railway labourer born Hope

There were also other railway labourers who were local men.

In the village of Penyffordd, there were two passenger railway stations, Hope and Penyffordd station was situated in the middle of the village and the second station, which still exists, was then named, Penyffordd for Leeswood. There were also smaller halts namely Hope Junction and Exchange Low Level.

Mrs Gwen Lloyd, a station porter .

Chester–Mold–Denbigh. L&NWR

The Mold Railway Company constructed a double track from Saltney Ferry to Mold, under the Act of 9 July 1847, opening on 14 August 1849.

The route began at Chester General Station, through Saltney Ferry, Broughton and Bretton stations, 4¾ miles from Chester. The line then continued to Kinnerton, climbing the stiff gradient (1 in 43 and 1 in 50), in fact freight trains had to be assisted, before swinging westerly to Hope and Penyffordd station. Here it crossed the Hawarden to Wrexham Road, where there was a level crossing with gates operated by the signalman. There were sidings on the down side for sixteen wagons, with a provision for a further six on the up side. The line then continued to Hope Exchange low level station. At this point the line passed under the other railway, the Wrexham, Mold & Connah's Quay line. The platform had a footpath to change trains, and a spur line off WM&CQ line formed a connection to the Mold railway track.

The earliest working timetables available were dated August 1862, for passenger and goods between Mold and Chester General Station. It was not until 1905 that a proposal for a footbridge was put forward, to be placed in the village, close to the village school.

Hope Exchange high and low levels were closed on 30 April 1962. The Denbigh, Mold and Chester line closed to passengers on 2 September 1963.

The Wrexham, Mold & Connah's Quay Railway

This railway was opened for passenger traffic on 1 May 1866. These trains ran from Wrexham to Mold and Buckley, stopping at Gwersyllt, Cefnybedd, Caergwrle, Hope Junction and Mold. The bus took passengers to Buckley. Note that the Penyffordd station did not open until August 1877. The train stopped at Hope Junction in order that passengers could change to the L&NWR railway below (hence the label 'low level'). At this time, in 1866, the traffic managers office was in the Hope Chambers at Wrexham.

Even in this first month of May the popularity of the railway was such that extra trains had to be run on Saturdays; these left Buckley at 2.45 *p.m.* and Wrexham at 9 *p.m.*, only 1st and 2nd class were issued, 3rd class tickets were restricted to market days, and dubbed 'market tickets' (issued for Mold market on Wednesdays and Saturdays, on fair days and to Wrexham market on Thursdays and Saturdays). The first train during the week was the 9.40 a.m. from Wrexham, arriving at Mold 10.40 *a.m.* The fares were charged according to which class you

travelled in. First class for the whole journey to Mold was 2*s.* 6*d.*, 2nd class 1*s.* 9*d.* and 3rd class 1*s.* 4*d.* At this time there were three trains per day each way. This was a time of horse-buses, however it is not clear where these were used. The steam engine began and ended the day at Buckley, and so the engine driver and crew would have been based there.

Hope Junction signal box, 1956. Note Hope High level station in the distance. The track on the left links to the Low Level Mold line.

Top Right: The platform sign at Penyffordd High Level station (showing Penyffordd for Leeswood), c.1914.

Bottom right: Locomotive M4065 pulls a passenger train out of Hope Exchange Low Level station. [W. A. Camwell, The Stephenson Locomotive Society]

Below: Porter, Rees Leek and Billy Hughes loading coal in the sidings at Hope & Penyffordd station, 1940.

There were cattle pens and another siding at Penyffordd behind the up platform, and because it was such an important centre of traffic for WMCQ purposes, it was served by a crane which could lift up to one ton. The mineral businesses, such as the coal mines of Llay, Rhosddu, Gresford, etc., descended onto the LNWR (Chester–Mold line), and from there they reversed and made their way to Chester and on into England.

There had been more plans for the area surrounding Penyffordd station. The Act of 1862 meant that railway number 2 was to commence on the Mold branch of the Chester–Holyhead line in order to connect trains coming from Mold with the WMCQ. This would have been ideal for the heavy coal traffic which came from the Mold area, thus enabling coal to be shipped overseas from Connah's Quay. However, for some reason, this plan was abandoned and so it became known as the lost chord!

After 1870 and the start of a half day a week free time plus the Bank Holiday Act with the increase in annual holidays, manual workers had more leisure time. With the advent of the railways there were opportunities to travel to the countryside from Liverpool. Caergwrle became a popular place to visit; special tickets enabled visitors to enjoy their days out. The London & North Eastern Railway produced a book called *Rambles around Caergwrle* written by T. Lloyd Jones. Walks and rambles around our villages are clearly described, here is just one:

CHEAPER FIRST CLASS FARES

The First Class Fares shown throughout this publication have been reduced to 50% over the corresponding Third Class Fares

CHEAP DAY RETURN TICKETS

ANY TRAIN — ANY DAY

(Subject in all cases to a return service being available the same day)

FROM	Rambles Nos. 1 to 9 Caergwrle Castle		Ramble No. 10 Hawarden	
	1st Class	3rd Class	1st Class	3rd Class
Bidston	4/5	2/11	3/3	2/2
Birkenhead Park	4/8	3/1	3/8	2/5
Blacon	2/3	1/6	1/6	1/–
Buckley Junction	–/9	–/6	–/5	–/3
Burton Point	2/3	1/6	1/3	–/10
Caergwrle Castle	—	—	1/2	–/9
Cefn-y-bedd	–/3	–/2	1/3	–/10
Chester (Northgate & Liverpool Rd.)	1/6	1/–	1/2	–/9
Connah's Quay & Shotton	1/8	1/1	–/6	–/4
Gwersylt	–/8	–/5	1/8	1/1
Hawarden	1/2	–/9	—	—
Hawarden Bridge Halt	1/9	1/2	–/6	–/4
Heswall Hills	3/3	2/2	2/2	1/5
Hope Village	–/3	–/2	1/2	–/9
Liverpool (Landing Stage)	5/2	3/5	4/–	2/8
Liscard and Poulton	4/6	3/–	3/6	2/4
Neston and Parkgate	2/9	1/10	1/8	1/1
Pen-y-ffordd	–/8	–/5	–/9	–/6
Saughall	2/3	1/6	1/2	–/9
Seacombe & Egremont	4/11	3/3	3/9	2/6
Sealand	1/11	1/3	–/11	–/7
Storeton	3/6	2/4	2/5	1/7
Upton	4/–	2/8	2/11	1/11
Wrexham (Exchange and Central)	–/11	–/7	2/2	1/5

CONDITIONS OF ISSUE

Tickets are issued subject to the Company's Byelaws, Regulation thd Conditions. These are not printed in this book but they appear in the Company's book of General Time Tables and in the Book of Regulations relating to traffic by Passenger Train, copies of which can be inspected at any station.

Railway fares for the 'Rambles' from Caergwrle Castle and Hawarden.

ROUTE OF RAMBLE No. 14

PEN-Y-FFORDD, TOWN DITCH, CEFN-Y-BEDD

7 MILES.

Cheap Walking Tour Tickets issued every day by any train

Outward to Pen-y-ffordd

Returning from Cefn-y-bedd

	1st Class	3rd Class
Liverpool (Landing stage) ...	5/9	3/6
Seacombe & Egremont ...	5/7	3/4

Leaving Pen-y-ffordd station turn left along the road. Shortly after passing the first lane on the right cross a stile on the right to a field which skirts by the right of the lane ...

There is a detailed description of the route, followed by:

The village of Pen-y-ffordd lies about half a mile east of the railway station. Due to its salubrious situation, to which the presence of one of the North Wales sanatoria bears testimony, the village is rapidly expanding, but unfortunately it is in the nature of ribbon development, a growing practice strongly disapproved by lovers of the countryside.

One of Gladstone's favourite excursions in his carriage was the drive through Pen-y-ffordd to the junction with Hope road ...

Nature lovers will find it a particularly interesting hunting ground, for it abounds in wild life. From the neighbouring coverts you may catch sight of the slinking brown form of Reynard as he sets forth on one of his predatory expeditions, or you may be fortunate enough in seeing his frolicking cubs. From the trees you may hear the hoot of an owl or the calls of some of our less common wild birds, and in the reed beds you may find some of the most beautiful of our avian visitors ...

Many other outings were enjoyed by the villagers, for instance the United Choir of Penyffordd arranged picnics to Loggerheads, they left Hope and Penyffordd station about 1 p.m. bound for Rhydymwyn where they alighted, walking the rest of the way. They returned by brake to Mold then by train to return to the village at 8 p.m. (1905).

The trains were also used for daily journeys. In 1912 a report in the *Welsh Advertiser* said that a proposal had been made to the Great Western Railway on the Wrexham Mold & Connah's Quay line to stop the 8.25 a.m. train at Hope village and Penyffordd station for the convenience of Hawarden County School scholars, they were also asked to alter times of the trains for the steelworkers from Shotton who would then have to liaise with London and North Western for connections.

In the early 20th century the sidings were extremely busy. They were used by the coal industry and it was here that the local coalmen collected their coal. They were very busy as 6 coal merchants unloaded coal wagons there. Billy Hughes, Billy Davies, Bill Cunnah, Lawrence and William Edwards. The coal came from Llay Main and the Gresford colliery on the other line and was shunted along the Penyffordd line via Hope Exchange station.

Agricultural activities were also important. There were pens for holding cattle and sheep. Local farmers brought milk and eggs and tomatoes, *etc.* to be sent to Chester market. Often these goods were brought by horse and cart to the station. The Cambrian Oil Company also used the railways.

During the Second World War trains powered by American locomotives transported ammunition from Marchweil and Rhydymwyn to Husskinson docks in Liverpool. People were afraid that the Germans might try to bomb these trains and we have been told that the engine would stop under a bridge in order to prevent the enemy seeing the sparks and smoke.

Railway Accidents

Accidents were inevitable; these were reported in the *Welsh Advertiser* and other local papers.

One report in the local newspaper described a serious accident at Hope Junction (later to be called Exchange). On 2 September 1911 a nun was badly injured, according to the newspaper report, illustrating the danger of the use of level crossings. It appears that two sisters, from the Little Sisters of the Poor at Birkenhead, had changed from the Seacombe line (WM&CQ) to board the Mold train, which was waiting at the station. They crossed the level crossing, when the 5.45 *p.m.* from Mold, approaching from the opposite direction, knocked down Sister Martin. Unfortunately the wheels passed over her arm. The waiting train to Mold transported her to Mold Cottage Hospital where her arm was amputated, fortunately however she did recover.

On 27 December 1913, a goods train was derailed at Hope Junction causing a delay of 1¹/₂ hours.

A fatal accident occurred in 1915 when 48 year old Thomas Wright of the Bannel, an employee at Rhosddu Colliery in Wrexham left work 5.30*p.m.* to return home. His body was found on the line by John Steel 600 yards from Hope Exchange on the way to Buckley Junction. Wright was evidently walking home on the line when he was struck by a train; there was a wound on the side of his head. He left a wife and eight children, one of whom was serving with the colours at the front in the First World War.

Another accident which occurred to Herbert Thomas, the young son of Mr & Mrs Edwin Thomas, who was playing on the railway footbridge by Penyffordd school and fell down some steps injuring his head and arm rather seriously. He was also bleeding profusely from a head wound. Dr Tudor Williams of Caergwrle was summoned and the newspaper reported that he was progressing favourably.

The railways certainly had a profound effect on village life, not only bringing in outsiders from all over the country but also enabling easier and more convenient contact with the other towns and villages. They also played an important part in villages activities, day trips, holidays and work became more accessible.

The Penyffordd 'flyer' created great excitement when steaming through the village, particularly for the schoolchildren. If you stood on the footbridge smoke did get in your eyes, whilst in the earlier days the gates at the level crossing gave horses a well earned rest before tackling the Vounog Hill.

One resident from Penymynydd recalls that if she heard the train blow its whistle coming up the steep incline from Kinnerton she had just enough time to run to Penyffordd station!

The advent of the omnibus was a welcome sight. Davies's buses ran from Wrexham to Buckley. It was 1d to ride from Derby Park Farm on the Wrexham road to Penyffordd School.

The first taxi service in the village was owned by Joseph Hewitt, a motor car proprietor, of Wood Lane Farm, Penyffordd.

Early Telegraphy

The electric telegraph ran alongside the railway track (as can be seen on the map). which allowed for the transmission of written or printed messages by electrical signals in Morse code, which was developed in 1837 before the telephone.

The Rebecca Riots and the Chartist Movement of the Mid Nineteenth Century

In 1834 the new Whig government's decision to amend the Poor Law exacerbated an already critical time. Since 1815 poverty had been endemic in rural Wales, even though various attempts had been made to assist those who were in desperate need. The Poor Law Amendment Act stated that outdoor relief would cease, parishes were to be grouped into unions, each with a Board of Guardians and workhouses were to be built. The population greeted this Act with contempt and outrage, as they continued to suffer.

The 1840s were known as the 'Hungry Forties'. 1842, in particular, suffered the worst economic depression known. The poor were at the end of their tether, desperate for food and in need of hope. The familiar images of Christianity no longer appealed, militant feelings grew and ran parallel to the demands of the Chartists, a group of campaigners for political reform whose demands were laid down in the People's Charter, published on 8 May 1838. Their main demands were for the vote to be given to all adult males, the introduction of a secret ballot, the payment of Members of Parliament (thereby allowing anyone to stand for election) the reorganisation of constituencies, the abolition of all property qualifications and annual Parliaments. The division between the social classes widened, the working class and underclass becoming the oppressed majority in the mid-nineteenth century. Radical freethinkers believed that Christianity was the root of all evil and held nothing for working class people.

Working class people and the poor, as they became better educated, wanted more than food and political representation. Christianity was not fulfilling the needs of any part of society, young, old, intellectual or uneducated and fear was being used as a form of social control. This was a serious moral problem, certain aspects of the Christian religion revealed double standards and hypocrisy. Historians argue that there were no Chartist activities in the area of Penyffordd and Penymynydd, however, it could be argued there was considerable Chartist sentiment in the region.

The second government decision which antagonised Welsh society was the Tithe Commutation Act of 1836. Since time immemorial the Church had been able to claim a tithe (one tenth) of all products produced on the land. Up until this time the tithe had been paid in kind *e.g.* one tenth of a grain crop; in many parts of Wales the Church had sold the tithe rights to laymen. This new Act meant that tithes would, in future, have to be paid in cash, based upon an agreed value of the estimated income from their land averaged out over a period of seven years. At a time of depression and extreme poverty in the countryside it was seen as a cruel blow. In a land where Nonconformity was fast overtaking the Anglican faith, this 'tax' was strongly objected to.

A third cause for rural discontent was the charges being made by the turnpike trusts for the movement of stock and other agricultural products. In west Wales this resulted in the outbreak of the so-called 'Rebecca Riots' where groups of men (dressed as women and calling themselves 'The Daughters of Rebecca') attacked and destroyed toll-gates. By 1843 their influence was spreading to north-east Wales.

It is argued that there was 'Rebecca' activity in Flintshire, and local residents have informed us that there could have been activity in Penyffordd at Rhos-y-brwyner Farm. However we have been unable to substantiate this information.

A letter in the *Chester Chronicle* written on 8 September 1843 shows that sympathy for the Rebecca movement was certainly affecting this area:

Sir,

The question of your correspondent 'Rebecca' in your last paper has often suggested itself to everyone accustomed to travel between Chester and Wrexham, three gates with high tolls in 11 miles is a grievance which might be shared surely with South Wales. Farmers have many sympathisers amongst us. Although there are no gates for 6 miles on the road nearest Wrexham, every other outlet of the town is protected by them with numerous sidebars which press very heavily on the humble industrious classes, which earn a scanty support by the coal traffic of your city. Many of these side bars are of recent erection and I think of doubtful legality, for once riding through one branching off the Mold road I declined paying of toll and gave the keeper my address in order to try the question but I heard no more about it. I have seen something of the road trusts in Wales and I assure you that the system is corrupt and expensive.

There are, however, records of Rebecca riots near Ruthin and Corwen.

The Churches of Penyffordd and Penymynydd

For many years religion had been the central influence in people's lives, and was at the forefront of education, in fact church attendance was compulsory until the Toleration Act of 1689.

During the Victorian Period (1837–1901) Christianity in Britain undertook an important change, partly because of social and economic pressures, and partly because of an enormous increase in the growth of the population. There were new and revived forces within organised religious life itself especially with the growth of the Evangelical movement.

The presumption had been that throughout Britain all people were committed members of the Anglican Church, attending regularly. This was not the case, as Horace Mann's religious census of 1851 proved.

Up to the beginning of the 19th century the inhabitants of our villages would have either attended the churches at Hawarden or Hope.

Hawarden Parish, although sited within the diocese of St. Asaph, did not belong to that ecclesiastic authority, it was a 'peculiar' attached to the Isle of Man (one of the Glynne's was made bishop there). The Rector was exempt from the jurisdiction of any bishop and so held its own church court, called a Consistory Court. In 1640 Elizabeth Gill of Pentrobin was presented there for having committed adultery with John Thomas of Northop, while in 1724, John Catherall of Pentrobin, was up for having sex out of wedlock with Ann Hewitt of Ewloe. On 29 September

St. John's Church, Penymynydd, c.1910

1639 Edward Mitolds of Pentrobin 'broke the Sabbath' 'for cominge as burden upon a dragge (sled) with a horse or mare ... (it) being Sunday the feast day of Michael the Archangel.' In 1637 Thomas Jones was sited for 'labouring in his garden and baking bread on a Sunday.'

It was customary, at this time, for the parish's godmothers to bake three-cornered cakes on All Saints Day (1 November) and present these to their godchildren during that evening. They also chanted:

> A soul a soul,
> a God of my soul.
> One for Peter
> And two for Paul,
> Three for them that makes us all
> To pray good dance a soul calls

(NLW Glynne of Hawarden, MS 184)

The opening years of the nineteenth century saw a great many changes within the established Church, a church under threat from the various Nonconformist denominations.

Rector Neville came to the living of Hawarden in 1814, and this was the beginning of a new state of affairs for this parish. The new Rector realised his obligation to the distant hamlets in the parish and before many years he

Various interior views of St. John's Church showing the decoration which adorns all parts of the building.

erected schools and parsonage houses followed by churches in Broughton and Buckley, both with resident curates. Archdeacon Thomas of St. Asaph, in *The History of Diocese of St Asaph* , writes that these churches were pioneers of the great work. The new parish of Buckley was created in 1874, from the township of Ewloe Wood and part of the townships of Ewloe town and Pentrobin.

The Church of St. John the Baptist, Pentrobin

The church of St. John the Baptist is situated in the parish of Hawarden, within a few yards of its boundary with the parish of Hope. It was built by Sir Stephen R. Glynne at a cost of £2,000, and consecrated on 22 July 1843. It is still considered to be an outstanding example of Victorian architecture, with its gothic arches, extremely ornate interior and perfectly proportioned spire. The wonderful murals depicting the stages of the life of Christ (it is said that these paintings were copied from pictures by the German artist Overbeck) adorn the stonework. They were a labour of love by the first curate the Rev. John Ellis Troughton, who was curate for 21 years. He also designed the stained glass windows. The story of Christ has been brought to life by his outstanding work for generations of parishioners of Hawarden and Pentrobin. The paintings were renovated by W. H. Gladstone in 1889–90 and the rest of the walls in 1893–4.

Tom Cropper, the historian from Buckley, wrote that this was a pretty little country church, and noted that there was a central aisle which had meant the men and boys sat on the right and the women and girls to the left. This was an ancient custom, which was adopted when the church was built. It apparently became a standing joke, as you entered the church on the women's side were the words — 'Come unto me ye blessed', ending on the men's side with 'Depart from me you cursed!'

Alongside the church is the graveyard, a record of the graves has recently been published. The lych gates were dedicated to the memory of Thomas Henry Ashcroft, from Liverpool who was killed at the crossroads 1 October 1911. The church clock was a gift from Mrs Wickham in 1908.

The church celebrated its 150th anniversary in 1993 with the Archbishop of Wales, Alwyn Rice-Jones.

During the depression of the 1930s the church provided soup kitchens for the poor.

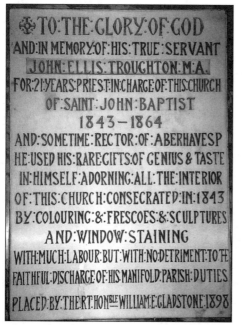

Emmanuel Church, Penyffordd

Emmanuel Church was opened in 1959 and was designed on the lines of Wrexham's War Memorial Hospital Chapel, at the special request of Mr George Leech the churchwarden who had been a patient there. The church council visited Wrexham and agreed the design. It was built at a cost of £3,750, by Shones on land that had been bought from Mr T. J. Scott of Osbourne House.

The Anglican Church had, however, been established in the village many years previously. Francis Aylmer Frost, son of Meadows Frost of Meadowslea, set up the mission church in the 1870s in an old building between Chester Road and the Old Road to Penymynydd. According to one historian, a visitor might have been struck by its diminutive size and

The memorial tablet to the Rev. J. E. Troughton in St. John's Church.

Above and right, two sketches of the 'Tin Church'. The small building shown above was replaced in 1890 by the 'second-hand' building shown on the right.

Above, a local taxi at the side of the 'Tin Church'.

Above, some of the stained glass work in the present-day Emmanuel Church, Penyffordd.

Left: The altar at Emmanuel Church, Penyffordd.

Above, the Emmanuel Church, Penyffordd, War Memorial.

Emmanuel Church, Penyffordd, 2002.

unpretentious exterior, but would have been agreeably surprised upon entering to find everything so becoming to a House of God. There was a communion table, over which was a stained glass window representing our Saviour blessing little children; a suitable pulpit, harmonium and comfortable seats for the congregation.

Francis A. Frost conducted services here for ten years and established a Sunday school, Bible classes and a choir, until he left the district in 1888 after being ordained by the Bishop of Chester. He was fondly remembered. After his departure evil days befell the church — the congregation had to leave but they did not dissolve. It is unclear as to what happened during this time, however Mr Pugh of the Church Army carried on the good work, led by the Rev. J. Rowlands (Rector of Hope), Mr Durdon (another energetic Church Army worker) and various Sunday school teachers. In 1889 services and Sunday school were held regularly in a room lent by Mr Wilkinson at The Beeches and in 1890 a new church was opened at the cost of £240 8s. 11d. This was an iron church, purchased from Pen-y-groes, near Caernarfon.

The opening service was attended by the Rev. Frost and Rev S. E. Gladstone. It was known locally as the 'Tin Church', and had a strong branch of the Temperance Society (Band of Hope, 1915).

In 1909 a new church scheme was set up to build a new church to replace the Tin Church. It was to be many years however before this was built. The Bishop of St. Asaph, Dr. D. D. Bartlett, consecrated the new Emmanuel Church on St. Barnabas' Day, 11 June 1959.

The Church has an active role in the village and regularly holds coffee mornings; there is also a Women's Guild, which was formed in 1984.

Nonconformity

The passion and vitality of the evangelical revival in the late 18th century and early 19th century and their missionary zeal, touched all aspects of the public and private life of virtually every man, woman and child, not only on Sundays but also throughout the week.

By the 1840s these changes had resulted in the establishment of many voluntary bodies such as Sunday schools which opened the door to literacy and learning, and often a lifetime's attachment to a particular church or creed.

Griffith Jones (who died in 1761) set up 'Circulating Schools' which it is claimed made half the Welsh population literate. His schools were clearly successful and S.P.C.K. Sunday Schools were launched in 1787 by Robert Raikes and Hannah More. Other voluntary bodies such as Bible classes and the Boys Brigade not only served to educate people but also promoted Christianity,

The wooden eagle lectern at Emmanuel Church, Penyffordd.

catering for the spiritual and physical needs of the working class and poor.

John Wesley's great revival movement, which began in 1738 when he was 35, was split by several trends of thought and, towards the end of the 18th century, six years after his death, a number of people left the established Methodist Church. This group was led by Alexander Kilham and became known as the Methodist New Connexion. Others who later followed this lead, were the Primitive Methodists in 1810, the Bible Christian Methodists and the Wesleyan Methodists. In 1857 the Wesleyans formed the United Methodist Free Church. The fervent spread of Methodism inevitably reached the localities of Penymynydd and Penyffordd.

The Penymynydd Methodist Church

The first mention of Penymynydd, according to C. Duckworth, occurred in the plan of Chester Wesleyan Circuit in 1701.

In Penymynydd small groups of people had already begun to meet regularly practising the new Methodist form of worship in various places such as barns, stone cottages, or wherever there was shelter. It was recognised that a permanent place of worship was essential with this fast growing membership and enthusiasm. A plot of land was acquired and work was carried out by local people, even the children helped by carrying stones from the nearby quarry to the site. The new chapel was founded in 1824, upon rock both materially and spiritually. There was a stove in the middle of the floor, which burnt coal and wood, and oil lamps provided the lighting.

The chapel became known as Mount Tabor, and was in the Hawarden Circuit of the Methodist New Connexion. There is little recorded evidence concerning the life of the church.

In 1907, the Wesleyan's, the Bible Christians and the Methodist New Connexion joined forces and became part of the United Methodist Church. The first building became unsafe and so Mount Tabor had to be rebuilt and re-opened on 7 Dec 1913. Sadly many of the young men who had worked so hard by quarrying the stone out of solid rock were to perish in the Great War of 1914.

Tom Cropper, an historian from Buckley, in his book *Buckley and District*, describes his visit to this chapel in 1923 when he was suitably impressed with the alterations — 'a quiet neat ordinary place of worship'.

There was a modernisation of the chapel in 1927 when central heating and electricity replaced the stove and oil lamps and it celebrated its 150th anniversary in 1974, when the feeling was that there was still much to do in the community. Unfortunately, twenty years later, in the autumn of 1994, the chapel closed.

In June 1839 there had been plans to build an English Primitive Methodist Chapel on the land held by Mr Griffiths of Stryt Isa, however, for some reason, this did not materialise.

The Penyffordd Methodist Church

The establishment of the first Methodist mission to Penyffordd came later. The Souvenir Booklet for the Veterans Rally published on 6 May 1914 tells how the men of Alltami and Buckley shared the honour of introducing Primitive Methodism to Penyffordd. Joseph Arrowsmith and Edward Davies (one of founders of the Buckley Jubilee) are remembered for holding open-air meetings in Penyffordd during the summer of 1852.

A small chapel had been built but had been abandoned, owing to a defective title to the site. Land was bought from farmer James Wright and the Primitive Methodist Chapel was built in 1855.

A plaque in the chapel shows the name Edward Bellis who was the honoured father of the Buckley and Deeside circuit. He had been converted when Penyffordd was missioned in 1852, and immediately attached himself to the cause and its interests, becoming a local preacher two years later, preaching 'homely, simple and experimental

Left: William Davies outside Mount Tabor, the Penymynydd Methodist Church, pre 1913.

Below: Mount Tabor Chapel members, 1910.

Below: The newly rebuilt Mount Tabor Chapel in 1913.

Above: Interior of Mount Tabor Chapel.

Left: The membership of Mount Tabor Chapel pose outside for a photograph, c.1929.

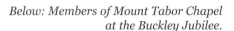

Left: Sunday School outing, Mount Tabor, c.1929.

Below: Members of Mount Tabor Chapel at the Buckley Jubilee.

sermons aptly illustrated' which were well received. Included in the booklet are the names of other stalwarts linked to the church at this time, Peter Wilcock, Peter Wainwright and Margaret Bevan.

The cause continued to grow, and by 1870 it was agreed that more room was needed. In 1872 a new chapel was opened having been constructed alongside the old building. The original chapel became the schoolroom and was the venue of the village elementary school for a short period from 1875–76.

In 1921, the addition of a vestry and porch linked the two buildings and at the same time two stained glass windows were presented in memory of those who had fallen in the First World War. The following year, in a complicated transaction, the trustees bought a further piece of land from the Hewitt family — the trustees paying £50 and Emma Louise Frost of Rhosbryner Farm £15. This was land on which the two chapel villas were built.

A report in the *Primitive Methodist Leader* describes the opening and dedication of the new pipe organ in 1925 in memory of Samuel Bevan and Margaret Bevan.

Zion Presbyterian Chapel

The origin of the Zion Presbyterian Chapel dates back to 1840, when Thomas Evans, a farmer in Hope, commenced the cause of Zion. He rented a thatched barn on Lower Mountain, two miles from Hope, to begin a Sunday school and for preaching the gospel. In *Home Missionary* for July 1842 it is recorded that there were at Zion seven members and fifty-four children at Sunday school. A busy,

Penyffordd Methodist Church and vestry, 1930s.

Left: Opening the new annexe at Penyffordd Methodist Church, 1921. L–R: John Bevan, Annie ?, Mrs Maria Astbury, Mrs Margaret Bevan, Mrs Jane Astbury, Mr Ted Bevan, Mr William Bevan

Below: The re-opening of the Penyffordd Methodist Church, October 1958. Rev. Blainey, Rev. Daniel, Mrs Adeline Parry, Rev. Trevvet.

Illuminated address to Mrs Margaret Bevan, 1921.

Below: The organ at Penyffordd Methodist Church, 2002.

Below: Trinity Chapel, 2000. [Capabilities]

dedicated farmer, Evans had six children and a farm to manage. The church prospered and his sons, David and Benjamin, carried on the work. David was made a deacon. The Rev. W. Smith took charge of Rossett, Burton, Bethlehem and Zion from the year 1854. The congregation at Zion increased despite the accommodation being poor, the building being small, cold and damp. When on one occasion a Welsh Minister was preaching the snow came across the room, he remarked, 'If Zion above is no better than Zion below, I have no desire to go there'.

At a church meeting in 1864, the Rev. E. Powell and the Pastor, the Rev. J. Meredith, proposed that a new chapel should be built. A site was chosen on the Vounog Hill, given by Mr Joel Williams of Mold for a nominal sum of five shillings, paid to make the title sure. A Mr Craig, generously undertook to be both the architect and builder and also giving a donation.

Young people formed a Bible class in the early 20th century as well as a Band of Hope. The church was described by a local newspaper as being in a flourishing state. In 1928 electric lighting was installed to replace the old oil lamps.

On the 25 April 1934 the new church hall was opened. This had a stage and seating for well over a hundred people. In 1936 the church and Sunday school performed a 'Grand Operetta'. Many other similar events took place in the 1930s.

Zion Chapel survived many years from 1854–1990, an evacuee family being housed in the schoolroom there during the Second World War. It was a sad day when it was demolished.

A New Church

It was announced in August 1994 that there was to be a new church in Penyffordd. The villages of Penyffordd and Penymynydd agreed that the three churches, Zion (Presbyterian), Mount Tabor (Methodist) and Penyffordd Methodist would form Trinity Chapel, Penyffordd. This would be the first project of its kind in north Wales.

The Trinity Chapel would use the premises previously occupied by the

Zion Presbyterian Church.

Zion Chapel Players, 1948. Back row: ? Williams, Jane Brodie, James Butterworth. Front row: Dilys Bell, Joan Davies, Mary Butterworth, Phyllis Probert.

Flower arranging group at Zion Chapel.

Penyffordd Methodists. The opening service was on 9 October 1994. Trinity is now part of both the Methodist Church and the Presbyterian Church of Wales. It is known as a local ecumenical project, and is in the Buckley and Deeside Circuit of the Methodist Church as well as the Cheshire, Flint and Denbigh Presbytery of the Presbyterian Church of Wales; a challenging time for all.

There have been many alterations to modernise Trinity, providing a kitchen, renewing the sound system, and other facilities.

Trinity Chapel has an important role in both communities with the following activities: monthly Lunch Club, coffee mornings each Thursday, which are preceded on every other Thursday by prayer meetings. Open Door Fellowship and Craft and Literary Group on alternating Mondays. Pastoral visitors are able to call upon those unable to attend services. Each year members of the chapel join in the Buckley Jubilee. There is also a Sunday school which is now called 'Chi. Ps.' (Children's Praise). The community uses the schoolroom for Tai Chi.

The churches and chapels of Penyffordd and Penymynydd were certainly at the hub of these communities. It is fascinating to read about the dedicated people who brought Christian worship to this district, and their determination to build churches. The growth of these communal meeting places brought the villages together during the 19th century, indeed it could be said that the churches created the villages.

Even though two of our chapels have disappeared it is good to know that their spirit and commitment is still with us, moving into the 21st century and the Church of St John the Baptist, Emmanuel Church and Trinity Chapel are still an integral part of our community.

Education

Elementary education following the 1870 Education Act

By the middle of the 19th century there was widespread recognition throughout the country that education should be organised nationally. The industrial age required workers who could read, write and do simple mathematics. Gladstone's government was pledged to provide free elementary education for children and introduced the Education Act of 1870 which established schools which were to be run by locally elected school boards. Private schools and church schools were already in existence.

Penyffordd School

From 1875 to 1904 this school was under the authority of the Hope School Board with the Rev. F. R. Lloyd, Vicar of Llanfynydd, as Chairman, and Mr Peter Wilcock (of Penyffordd) as Vice Chairman (later Chairman).

Penyffordd School pupils and teacher, 1896.

In 1875, the newly elected Hope School Board decided to build a school in Penyffordd. Land was bought at a cost of £150 and, on 14 July, a contract was signed with Mr Bleakley of Birkenhead to build a school for 200 children at a cost of £1,440.

Whilst the school was being built a temporary school was established in what is now known as the School Room at Trinity Chapel. Elementary education therefore formally came to Penyffordd on 2 February 1875.

A log book had to be kept by schools on a weekly basis, however the Penyffordd School log books were written in daily by the headmaster, giving us a wonderful insight, not only into the subjects the children were taught, but also the state of the weather, harvesting times, agricultural trends (from potato picking to planting) and the prevalent diseases of the time which killed some children and badly affected others.

The first entry in the Penyffordd Log Book in 1875 was written by Mr John Brooks, the Headmaster, who came from Coedpoeth and remained as headmaster for 42 years until his retirement in 1917.

The first two names on the admission register were Jessie Bellis (who later emigrated to Australia and whose niece Mrs Annie Lewis was later cook at the school) and James Bell (whose son, also named James, became a teacher at Hawarden Grammar School). Other names included Ed Wilcock, age 10, and William Wilcock, age 11.

It was not until 14 June 1876 that the new school building was completed when the children formed a procession with members of the School Board to walk to the new school.

John Brook's salary, possibly for June to December, in this first year was £23 3s 9d. He worked alone initially but found this difficult. In 1878 his salary had increased to £120 and an assistant mistress had been appointed at a salary of £45, and one pupil teacher who was paid £10. As the numbers on the roll increased the headmaster was helped by an assistant lady teacher and two monitors who were senior scholars. Even so classes were large and discipline strict. Teaching was very formal with an emphasis on the '3 Rs'. Classrooms were furnished with long desks with no backs which were set in rows. There was very little equipment and slates were

Penyffordd School.

used for writing on, especially in the infant classes. The school was frequently inspected and a summary of the first inspection is as shown opposite.

These Inspectors had the power to recommend that part or all of the school grant could be withheld if they were not satisfied by the standard being achieved.

Music and singing was introduced into the Penyffordd Council School curriculum in December 1877. Other subjects on the timetable consisted of spelling, writing, geography and poetry, examples of the latter being: *The Blind Boy* by C. Cibber; *The First Grief, Oh! Call my brother back to me* by Felicia Hemans; *The Village Blacksmith* by Longfellow. More subjects were introduced through-out the years.

The First Grief
Felicia Hemans

"Oh! Call my brother back to me,
I cannot play alone;
The summer comes with flower and bee–
Where is my brother gone?

The butterfly is glancing bright
Across the sunbeam's track;
I care not now to chase its flight–
Oh! Call my brother back.

The flowers run wild–the flowers we sowed
Around our garden tree;
Our vine drooping with its load–
Oh! Call him back to me."

"He would not hear my voice, fair child!
He may not come to thee;
The face that once like spring-time smiled
On earth no more thou'lt see.

A rose's brief life of joy,
Such unto him was given;
Go-thou must play alone, my boy–
Thy brother is in heaven!

"And has he left the birds and flowers,
and must I call in vain;
and through the long, long summer hours,
will he not come again?

And by the brook, and in the glade,
Are all our wanderings o'er?
Oh! While my brother with me played,
Would I had loved him more!"

In 1894/5 the following were taught to the kindergarten:

4 years old — building and beads
6 years old — matt weaving, pricking and embroidery
5 years old — frilling, letter forming

Top right: School Logbook entry for the opening of Penyffordd School, 1875.

Bottom right: A summary of the School Inspector's report on Penyffordd School, indicating that the teaching did not come up the the standard required for the allocation of the full grant.

Below left: School inspector's report for Penymynydd School, 1891 which is critical of the discipline and attendance of the pupils.

1875.

Dec 2nd Took charge of the Pen-y-ffordd Temporary Board. Admitted 26 Scholars - boys and girls. Took the greater part of the morning to examine and classify them, worked a little in the afternoon.

3rd One or two boys absent today - owing I suppose to the weather. Not much done today, most of the children having neither books nor slates. Mr Wilcock, vice-chairman of the Board visited the school.

4th As most of the children had brought slates; and many reading books - we were enabled to go through a little work. I find them to be pretty good readers, but are backward in Arithmetic.

5th The weather has been very severe all week. On enquiry I find that the few absentees we have had, has been occasioned by this. Satisfactory progress has not been made this week, owing to us having no blackboards or books belonging to the school.

396

Report for 1891

Mixed School "The Grammar of the sixth and seventh standards, and the Geography of the third and fourth standards were very poor, I was pleased with the Grammar of the fifth standard and with some of the maps. The standard work was fair; the style of the paper work and the Arithmetic vivâ voce need considerable attention. The master should have had all things in readiness for the Examination. Though improved, I have still some hesitation in recommending the full grant for discipline. The musical drill was very pleasing Infts Class. Some good work is done in this class: the infants were very nicely behaved, some low desks are advisable. The average attendance should be improved".

A. H. Collins is recognised under Art 68.
B. Jones (Candidate) Failure "

John H Watinough
Manager

Summary of the Inspector's Report on the school.

"This is still a new school and the children have not yet got over habits of Copying and prompting which greatly affect both discipline and instruction. The first class are fairly well taught. The Elementary work below this is poor, and Geography and Grammar fail throughout. Allowance however must be made for illness during the early winter. The part singing is very creditable. More books are wanted.

Improvement must be looked for next year as a condition of an unreduced grant (Art. 32 (b))

H.M. Inspector is unable to recommend payment of the Grant under Art. 19 (c) 3 on account of the defective discipline.

A programme for an evenings entertainment at Penyffordd Board School, 1 February 1887.

The infants also learned nursery rhymes.

The summer provided some light relief and half days were given for various reasons. One such was the annual flower show held in school, another time there was the Hartsheath Festival. Sunday School day trips to various destinations such as Rhyl, Eaton Hall, Loggerheads and New Brighton on the Wirral, meant more days off school. The three Sunday Schools from the Nonconformist chapels had held their trips on different days thus disrupting the children's school attendance. The headmaster complained bitterly about this and asked for the trips to be either planned for the same day or to be organised during the holidays. In June 1891 a competition was held and prizes given for the best bouquet of wild flowers; the bouquets were sent to Chester Infirmary.

Children were often kept away from school to help with farming and domestic activities. Boys were required for hay making and potato picking, the harvest, etc, and it is significant that today's school holidays appear to reflect times of potato picking, planting in February, hay making and harvest. Both sexes went blackberrying. Older girls were often kept at home to help their mothers. In 1898 Mr Brooks reported that there were a few pupils in Standard VI, who only attend school when there was nothing else for them to do at home. A glimpse of the outside world was brought into the school when a black man gave a talk on Jamaica using a magic lantern.

Not only were the events of the school recorded in the log books but a separate punishment book was kept from 1910–34. This study of the entries for 1910–17 is very revealing. Most punishments recorded were of strokes of the cane on the hand, rarely on the back.

Disobedience — 3 strokes on the hand
Carelessness — 2 strokes on the hand
Untruthfulness — 2 strokes on the hand
Unpunctuality — 2 strokes on the hand
Inattention — 2 strokes on the hand
Catching a train — 1 stroke on the hand
Disobeying a teacher — 4 strokes on the hand
Climbing trees — 4 strokes on the hand
Robbing birds nests & killing birds — 4 strokes on the hand
Insulting behaviour — 3 strokes on back

During the 1870s to 1890s illness was prevalent. In 1875 October diphtheria claimed the lives of at least four children, even the Headmaster caught the disease. Other diseases which affected the children were scarlet fever, scarletina, mumps, whooping cough and measles. An epidemic of measles is recorded in the Log Book in 1877 showing that more than ten children suffered. Most epidemics appeared at wintertime and the Medical Officer of Health was forced to close the school down for several weeks until the epidemics had abated. During an outbreak

Standards 1 & 2, Penyffordd Council School, 8 June 1923, with the headmaster, Mr J. D. Parry.

of whooping cough in October 1899, Mr Brooks wrote, 'some children are not likely to attend again during the winter especially from the infant class'.

Epidemics persisted even into the 20th century. The school closed, however, for 14 days in 1917 due to a severe epidemic of whooping cough.

During 1919, 20 school children were variously examined by the school nurse, doctor and dentist. Some parents objected and threatened to send their children to another school. The dentist undertook treatment in the school but only 30% of parents allowed this treatment, even though Mr Parry (Headmaster 1917–42) advised that 'treatment should be compulsory'. Children's illnesses continued to be a problem with many losing time at school. Occasionally deaths occurred and everyone dreaded being taken to the Fever Hospital at Dobshill in the 'Fever Wagon'. The children in the top class were given lectures on temperance and the prevention of tuberculosis.

The weather appeared to be far more seasonal than it is today with hot summers and severely cold winters, and extremely wet weather during the springtime, which resulted in children being sent home to dry. The school could become very cold in the winter. Coal stoves, which stood unprotected in the class rooms were dangerous. A nasty accident was reported in 1882:

> Gave a half day holiday in the afternoon in order to have the school cleaned. One of the girls instead of going straight home, went to the classroom with one or two others to warm themselves, going I suppose , inside the stone coping, her dress caught fire. As it happened I and one of the teachers were in the other classroom so it was put out without any injury being done. I have asked for guards for the fireplaces since last week.

A Log Book entry in February 1892 highlights the problems caused by this intense cold —'the coldest day ever remembered, took singing and exercise too cold to write'. The headmaster had reason to complain in January 1885 that the fires had not been lit until late morning and therefore the school was very cold, the school cleaner had not attended to her duties. If coal was late being delivered to the school, as in 1905, the fires were not lit until 6 October. This meant that the infants had to be marched around the room at intervals to get warm!

In 1921 these old fires were replaced with slow combustion stoves and in 1935 central heating was installed, doing away with the coal stoves and unequal warmth.

It was not until August 1929 that Bellis & Griffiths installed electric lighting, even though the school had been connected to the mains since January, the building had not been wired up. On 28 November, the headmaster commented, 'a very dark foggy day, electric light a boon today'.

A well had been sunk in 1876 to provide the school with water and mains water was not supplied until early in the 20th century.

Outside, the schoolyard was often in a muddy state during winter and so in 1909 the yard was finally tarmaced after many complaints.

Concerns about where children could play were brought into sharp focus when a pupil, Reg Egerton, was summoned before the magistrates for playing football on the road. It appears that the Local Education Authority had refused to provide a playing field.

Conditions at the school often had to be remedied. In April 1900 the unstable condition of the bell spire gave cause for concern, and so the school was closed for a week while it was demolished. The bell had always been rung in the mornings to call children to school.

But worse was to come when a portion of the floorboards were removed to reveal a cesspool containing two-three inches of highly polluted stagnant water from the latrines. The school was closed for five weeks while this was remedied and, in addition to new block flooring, the walls were painted. As the local newspaper commented, 'parents will have no cause of complaint. '

In 1902 the new Education Act made the School Boards redundant and the monitoring and funding of the school was passed to Flintshire County Council. The school then became known as the Council School and was administered by School Managers.

Mr Brook's finally retired in 1917. He had been the headmaster for 42 years and had seen the school roll grow to 160 children, the school becoming an important focus for village activities. His replacement was Mr John Dickens Parry.

In October of his first year, Mr Parry started a gardening club where the boys were given instruction on how to grow vegetables. He utilised the piece of land adjoining the school to make a garden. This was during the First World War, however there is very little reference to the war in the Log Book. One comment in 1916 refers to the older boys who were busy in the potato fields due to a shortage of available men. A reference was made in the newspaper to the excellent knitting done by some of the older girls for the soldiers and sailors.

In 1918 the children were entertained by a conjuring and ventriloquist exhibition by discharged wounded soldiers, 150 attended. The Armistice in November 1918 justified a school holiday.

On 26 May 1919 Mr Brook's died and, on 29 May, scholars lined the school yard with heads bowed as the cortege passed for burial in Hope Church cemetery. A local newspaper reported that 'the gap in village life left by John Brooks will be difficult to fill'.

The new headmaster was finding plenty to complain about in his school, from desks slipping about due to dancing powder being used on the floor for village dances, to the habit of keeping girls at home on Friday to help with the cleaning.

During 1924 the school was renovated while the classes continued to operate, the Mr Parry noted that '[school] work [was] being carried on under wretched conditions'. In fact, the building underwent a partial transformation, corridors and a teachers' room being added, plus the lavatories were converted to water closets.

During 1925 County Library books were distributed to pupils and Welsh was taught for the first time to one class. The Inspector wrote that 'there is a pleasant tone to the whole school'. To end a good year for the pupils prizes, certificates and oranges were distributed on 24 December.

The following year cookery classes were started for older girls and boys. These were held at Hope school but some parents were unhappy and would not let their children face this long walk in the wet weather. A National Savings Scheme was started in the school and proved to be very popular, by 1929 £1,000 had been saved entitling the school to one day's holiday.

The onset of the Second World War certainly had its effect on the school. From 1940 onwards there was a steady intake of evacuees, from Wallasey, Birkenhead, Manchester and Liverpool. Most stayed only a few months. In September 1944 fifteen children arrived from London, some as young as five years, but by Christmas they had

The headmaster, Mr J. D. Parry, and boys at Penyffordd Council School in the school garden, c.1925.

returned home.

The school children took part in the war effort with enthusiasm, Salvage was collected and packed. Rose hips collected to make Vitamin C syrup, a $^1/_2$ cwt being picked in one afternoon! The school eventually had an air raid shelter and this was used by the ARP as their head-quarters, a control point in case of emergency.

The school garden was very productive providing greens for families. The boys paid two shillings towards seeds and each received the appropriate share of the produce. 'Dig for Victory' was essential everywhere.

In 1942 Mr Parry retired after serving as headmaster for 25 years. In 1943 an old scholar from the school, Mr R. L. Parry, became the new headmaster.

The school was an important centre for the village, a lending library was opened for both adults and children. After the war, evening classes became popular and by 1948 there were classes in leatherwork, shorthand, book-keeping, embroidery, choral music, orchestral music, dressmaking and drama, with up to 108 people attending.

The school lost its garden when the canteen was opened in March 1949 to supply dinners (costing 4d) to Penyffordd and Penymynydd schools. At this time 170 meals were prepared each day.

The Inspectors report of 27 March 1950 shows a strong emphasis remained on the 3 Rs, although music and art were also popular. The senior pupils attended a practical course in Hope for instruction in housecraft and woodwork.

Children took an examination to be accepted at Hawarden Grammar School, those who did not pass stayed on in school until the leaving age of 14 years. In later years those aged over 12 years went to the Secondary School at Shotton. In 1947 the leaving age was raised to 15 years and then 16 years in 1972. In 1953 the first intake of pupils from Penyffordd School went to the Elfed School in Buckley. Later that year, 11 year olds went to Castell Alun for two years then transferred to the Elfed School for the rest of their schooling. By 1971 this changed again and the pupils went to Castell Alun for full-time education.

In 1966 Mr R. L. Parry retired after being head for 23 years and his deputy, Mr J. R. Williams, was appointed headmaster. As many new houses were being built in the village the school intake rose. A mobile classroom was erected in the yard and the canteen doubled as a classroom in 1967.

Penyffordd Junior School and Abbot's Lane Infant School

As the village developed a new school was built on Penymynydd Road to accommodate the extra pupils. Even as the children moved in on 15 March 1971 the school was full and quickly became overcrowded. To solve this problem a second Infant/Junior school was built on Abbot's Lane which opened in 1977. The first headteacher

Mr J. D. Parry and pupils of Penyffordd Council School, 1932.

was Mrs Forrester.

In 1980 the local education authority decided that Abbot's Lane School would be for infants aged between five and seven years, while Penyffordd school would be for the junior pupils aged between seven and eleven years. Both schools had to be modified and later an extension was built at Abbot's Lane School.

After the retirement of Mrs Forrester in 1985, Mrs J. Griffiths took charge until 2001 when Mrs Westaway became the headteacher. In 1989, after nearly 30 years teaching in Penyffordd school, 23 of them as headteacher, Mr J. R. Williams retired and Mrs Pat Williams was appointed in his place. Both schools work very closely together and provide an excellent education for the children.

St. John the Baptist Voluntary Aided Primary School

Established in 1844 for the education of children in the principles of the Church of England this school was built on land donated by Sir Stephen Glynne to the Rector of the Parish of Hawarden. It stands close to St. John's Church on the Mold to Broughton road in Penymynydd.

A report from the Royal Commission on Elementary Education in Wales, 1847, gives a graphic description of the school which had one master and four monitors (who were changed weekly) providing an education to 58 boys and 51 girls. The master was paid £70 per annum (with a house and garden) while his wife taught the girls sewing. The Inspector found the children well behaved and very clean. They were well treated by the Master who had trained in Chester for one year, having formerly been employed in husbandry. He concluded that, the school room was healthily situated and altogether a very good one.

Pupils and staff at Penyffordd Council School, 1940s.

Children had to pay a weekly fee to attend the school. This is described as pence, however, for those who were too poor, the fee was paid — May 1886, Mr Hugh Roberts paid £1 5s. 8d. on account of seven pauper children up to 25 December ... A mother came to explain that her husband had been out of work for 18 weeks and would pay when he got employment. Some children were sent home having come to school without their pence and one boy was dismissed for great irregularity of payment. It was not until September 1891, following the Assisted Education Act, that, for the first time, children did not have to pay to attend school as a grant of 10s per head was paid in lieu.

Unfortunately early records of the school are not available and so we can only pick up the story of education in Penymynydd from the Log Books beginning in 1885 at a time when the attendance was 110–20 pupils and the master was a Mr Rogers when the Inspectors comments were: 'Miss Taylor could be a little more bright and cheerful with her charges'. The Inspector also drew attention to the close proximity of the lavatories to the main school, which seem to have been a source of concern for many years. In October 1896 the Sanitary Inspector declared the lavatories to be in a very bad state and ordered them to be cleaned. Earth closets were introduced in 1909 after which 'Cleaners to be seen regarding providing dry earth and sifted ashes in place of the mixture of ashes and cinders now supplied. Signed Harry Drew' (the son-in-law of William Ewart Gladstone, the Canon Drew School in Hawarden was named after him).

The school was closed for five or six weeks in 1907 in order to carry out alterations to the premises. The playground was fenced and divided for the sexes and asphalted; new blocks of offices were built and new cloakrooms were also erected. The classroom was transformed with improved lighting making it very pleasant. The long main room was divided with a sliding partition. The whole area was painted and decorated. The total cost of this renovation was about £1,000.

The school was heated with coal stoves fuelled by coal supplied by the Padeswood Colliery and later from the Wilcocks coalyard at Penyffordd station. There was often trouble with the school chimneys which smoked, so that windows had to be left open but, because of the cold weather, the children had to wear their hats on account of the draught.

Attendance at school was a great cause for concern, and an attendance officer visited regularly, sending notes to the children's parents. As with the school in Penyffordd, children were often kept at home to help in the home and in the gardens and also with potato picking, hay making, harvesting and blackberry picking. Sometimes children played truant as did William Wilcock who was found hiding in a pig sty! 13 May 1892. A few children absent no doubt owing to the races being held in Chester.

Occasionally children would leave the school playground to play in the woods or visit the local sweet shop, often returning late for school. A letter was sent to the local shops asking them not to provide sweets.

Penymynydd School, 1910.

In January 1888, a scheme was introduced to encourage better attendance. A ticket was given at the end of the week of full attendance and every three tickets got 1d at the end of the year. There is no record of whether this was a success.

Poor attendance often happened because of the terrible illnesses which frequently occurred in both villages such as whooping cough, measles and scarlet fever.

There seemed to be more poverty in this village than in Penyffordd as the headmaster noted 'poor attendance, some owing to want of boots, in the bad weather. '

There appears to have been a similar curriculum at Penyffordd School. We know that in 1897 the '3 Rs' were taught as well as sewing lessons and scripture. The Rev. J. H. Watmough gave scripture lessons on each Tuesday and Thursday morning. As this was a church school the emphasis was not surprisingly on religion, and so the children had to attend church on saint's days.

In 1888 there was a new headmaster — Mr Rogerson, an assistant mistress —Miss Reed, a pupil teacher —F. Davey, with two paid monitresses. Work was done on slates as the old headmaster had taken the pens with him — as they belonged to him! As with Penyffordd school there were often staff shortages and the headmaster would find himself teaching most of the pupils. Monitors were usually older pupils who had stayed on, and so had little training. One monitor was admonished for talking too much with the children and for hitting a child about the head.

Each year there was a religious knowledge examination by the Diocese Inspector. The Diocesan Report for September 1898 reads: 'This is a very good school. The teaching is thorough and effective and reflects much credit on the teachers'.

There seems to have been an effort to improve domestic and practical skills over the next few years — 'May 1912, Cookery classes were commenced for girls aged over twelve years and evening classes for girls who had left school (12 girls to attend in the evening unable to get 18 people for the day)'. In 1920 a gardening club was formed using the parsonage garden, and in 1921 Mr Percy Wood, the superintendent of manual training, came to the school and arranged for eleven boys to attend the Buckley centre for woodwork. There was a school football team, and matches were played against Broughton C of E school, Buckley St. Matthews, Bistre and, in 1921, a friendly match against Penyffordd Council School.

Penymynydd School, early 20th century.

There seem to have been many causes for celebration in late 19th century and early 20th century schools. On 2 June 1902, the Penymynydd School Log records that '... to celebrate the peace concluded with the Boers, the children were granted a holiday on Monday'.

Buckley Jubilee was celebrated, as there seems to have been a close affinity with Buckley, even in speech

Admission Number	Date of Admission			Re-Admission			NAME IN FULL (Surname First)		Evidence of Birth	Date of Birth			ADDRESS	NAME OF PARENT or GUARDIAN
	Day	Mth	Year	Day	Mth	Year				Day	Mth	Year		
1	23	4	1906				Hebbert	Gordon		21	4	01	Stony Hill	William
2	24	6	06				Astbury	Wm		11	6	01	Hawarden Rd.	William
3	8	7	06				Owens	Annie		18	7	01	Penymynydd	Thos.
4	22	7	06				Davies, Lu	Lily		23	6	01	" "	Edward
5	22	10	06				Connah Philip	Philip		27	8	01	Wood Lodge, Penterbu	Saml.
6	8	4	07				Thompson	George		24	9	01	Little Mountain	Alexander
7	9	4	07				Edwards	Florence		10	4	01	" " "	Edward
8	9	4	07				Gittens	Alice		6	1	03	" " "	William
9	29	4	07				Davies	Constance		27	2	02	Kinnerton Lane	John
10	30	4	07				Connah	John		27	8	01	Hawarden Road	Alfred
11	27	5	07				Bithell	Herbert		11	2	02	Stony Hill	Charles
12	8	7	07				Astbury	Kate		24	7	02	Hawarden Road	William
13	30	9	07				Owens	Alice		8	4	03	Penymynydd	Thos.
14	30	9	07				Rowlands	Alexander		19	2	03	Dob's Hill	Thomas
15	30	9	07				Davies, Ern	Ernest		26	7	02	The Warren	Arthur
16	2	12	07				Jenkins	Reginald		26	4	01	Penymynydd	Joseph
17	9	3	08				Meacham	Gladys		9	10	02	" "	Percy
18	7	9	08				Griffiths	Fredk.		3	10	02	Dirty Mile	Wm.
19	19	10	08				Gerrard	Florence		27	9	03	Water's Green	John
20	28	10	08				Jones	Henry		29	5	02	Dirty Mile	John
21	11	1	09				Price	Alfred		25	12	03	Penymynydd	Margaret
22	20	1	09				Catherall	William		6	12	03	" " "	Joseph
23	1	3	09				Ellis	William		8	12	03	" " "	Thos.
24	19	4	09				Crofts	John		6	8	03	The Warren	Albert
25	3	5	09				Astbury	Peter		28	5	04	Hawarden Road	Thos.
26	7	6	09				Connah	Alfred		9	3	04	" " "	Alfred
27	14	6	09				Thompson	William a		5	5	03	Little Mountain	Alexander
28	14	6	09				Davies	Emily		8	3	04	Kinnerton Lane	John Ll.
29	14	6	09				Meacham	John		6	6	03	Penymynydd	Percy
30	20	9	09				Ellis	Thomas		2	8	05	" " "	Thos.
31	20	9	09				Jenkins	Bessie	✓	8	6	05		Joseph
32	22	9	09				Connah	Samuel		6	6	04	The Lodge	Samuel
33	23	9	09				Wright	Clara		22	9	04	Bannel	Richard
34	1	12	09				Jones	Thomas		3	12	04	The Bannel	Thos.
35	7	3	10				Jenkins	F. Elizabeth		23	7	04	Penymynydd	Joseph
36	2	5	10				Astbury	Neville	✓	16	8	04	The Woo	Richard

Admission register, Penymynydd School, 1906.

i.e. the archaic words 'thee' and 'thou' were used in everyday speech.

On 14 October 1898 there was no school on account of the Barnum & Bailey Show which was billed as 'the greatest show on earth'. Possibly held at Wrexham or Chester, this huge American circus needed about four long trains to transport 400 horses, 20 elephants, camels, zebras, lions, Johanna the giant gorilla and 1000s of tons of curious creatures and creations. The show's tour of Great Britain was organised like a military operation staying only one or two days at each location. One can imagine the wonder and excitement of the children!

Royalty was certainly admired. Queen Victoria's Golden Jubilee was celebrated with a whole days holiday and 1562 children from the Parish of Hawarden attended the park at Hawarden Castle, in 1887. The Duke of York's wedding was celebrated with a fete at Hawarden in 1893.

On 15 May 1908, when the King visited Hawarden, a holiday was given so that the children could see him. There was a four weeks holiday in the summer which coincided with the harvest.

The punishment of school children was swift and harsh and was given for many reasons as can be seen from these accounts written in the Log Books: 1886 punishment of, 2 handers and 5 stripes on the back — for shouting out in school in order to make children laugh and for disobedience. In July Richard Astbury had a flogging for throwing stones in the school yard, cracking a window — his parents were told to pay for new one. Two children were punished for coming to school with rough hair. A boy who played truant by hiding in the pig sty received a flogging. In September 1888 children were cautioned for smoking and swearing!

One father who complained about his child's hand being swollen after punishment went away perfectly satisfied. A Mrs Connah, Pentrobin, also complained about the caning of her boy for being generally naughty and inattentive in class. She spoke of going to see the Rector and would not allow her son to come to school in the afternoon.

There are a few references to the Penymynydd 'roughs'.

Epidemics of measles, whooping cough, diphtheria and influenza often caused the school to be closed. There was an awareness of disease however, and in 1915 lectures were given on Laws of Health and prevention of tuberculosis. The school nurse attended in 1921 and children went to Penyffordd Council School to see the dentist.

During the Second World War, anti-gas and other Air Raid Precaution courses were held at the school. The building was also used as a Firewatch Post. Allotments were established near the school, as fresh food was desperately needed. Unfortunately the cows broke in!

It seems that practical and mental work was deemed important to the children of this school, and when they left school they were guided and advised. In 1919, the Choice of Employment Scheme for boys and girls leaving school was arranged by Flintshire Education Committee. A child could not be legally fourteen years until the end of term; there were three terms, Christmas, Easter and Midsummer. Just before the end of the term Mr Evans, a county officer would interview those about to leave regarding their choice of career.

It was suggested that the managers of each school should organise themselves into an After Care Committee for the district co-opting others to work with them on the committee. This committee should send a representative to sit on the local Hawarden, Shotton and District Choice of Employment Committees and also be a member of the Rota Committee. Various schools were arranged into groups within which each school elected a representative from its After Care Committee who together would form a Rota Committee which would meet Mr Evans at the end of each term, and with him visit all the schools of the group, interviewing those that were about to leave. The Rev. W. J. Rees was elected as the Penymynydd School representative on the District and Rota Committees.

A report by H.M. Inspector P. A. Lewis, dated 10 December 1940, covers many aspects of school life at this time. The accommodation consisted of two classrooms, the larger one divided by a glazed partition. Central heating, running water and electric lighting had been introduced in 1938.

The Headmaster, who had been appointed in 1919, took charge of the senior group. There were three assistants — a certificated male teacher, one uncertificated female teacher and one supplementary female assistant two of whom were experienced teachers. At this time there were 81 pupils on the roll. In 1935 there had been 108 on the register. Apparently increased housing provision in Hawarden had meant a decrease in pupils because of some migration from the Pentrobin district to Hawarden. Geography had been introduced on the curriculum and the male teacher had a rich collection of slides of Flintshire, made by himself, which were of great interest to the pupils. With a small film projector a wide collection of educational films were also shown. Music was also

Pupils and staff of Penymynydd School, 1950s.

important, the teacher of the infant section had successfully introduced a percussion band and folk dancing. Instruction in woodwork and domestic science was given at the Ewloe Green Practical Instruction centre. Other skills were taught such as bookbinding and weaving. Because of the war regular ambulance and first aid demonstrations were given.

This report praised the creative activities of the school. The Headmaster, himself a craftsman, could see the educational value of a practical approach to the study of these subjects. It seems the inspector was impressed by the school and satisfied with the standards achieved.

By 1950 the school roll had reduced even further to 39 pupils. The Diocesan Inspector's report classed the school as excellent.

Following the King's death in 1952 children listened to a radio broadcast describing his funeral. In 1953 the school closed for a week for festivities, celebrating the coronation of Queen Elizabeth II.

The school's outdoor toilet facilities were still very basic and it was not until April 1959 when the pail closets were converted to water closets. The state of the school buildings was a constant cause for concern. On the 17 March 1964 a letter was sent to the Rev. Baden-Powell from Flintshire Education Authority informing him of a proposal to close the school, and that the children were to be transferred to a proposed new school in Penyffordd because '… the school is unsuitable for improvement to bring it up to the standards required by the Ministry's regulations'. In July, objections were raised by the school managers who claimed that '… the school might well have another ten years of life … it is a thoroughly pleasant and happy school. It would seem to be a pity to close it'. On 31 July 1964 the Director of Education wrote that he had received information from the Department of Education that the proposed new school in Penyffordd was not included in the list of major projects, and so the school was reprieved.

The poor facilities had to be addressed, however, and in 1974 work started on a new extension to provide indoor toilets, a staff room and kitchen. Mr Dunn wrote that, contrary to expectations, the building workers did not unduly disturb the children.

The school roll began to grow and in 1975 there were 74 pupils. The following year Mr Dunn retired due to ill health and in September 1977 Mr G. M. Davies became the headteacher, introducing school uniform.

Housing development in Penymynydd has continued and to accommodate new pupils the school has undergone major re-modelling work, first in 1991 and then in 1997. In the second building phase the school had a first floor extension of two classrooms, an upper hall and a library.

The present Headteacher, Mr Byrne, ensures that the school provides a stimulating environment, where children receive a good education. For 159 years this has been the wish for all who have taught at St. John's

The pupils and staff of Abbot's Lane School, Penyffordd, 2000.

The pupils and staff of Penyffordd Junior Schoool, 2000.

The pupils and staff of St John's School, Penymynydd, 1999.

Pupils and staff of Penymynydd School, 1970s.

School. It has served the community well.

Private Schools

Annie Rodenhurst's School

In the 1871 census Annie Rodenhurst, the wife of a farm bailiff ran a private school in Penyffordd. It is possible that this was located in Beaconsfield Terrace, Hawarden Road. Reading, writing, arithmetic and embroidery were taught. The fee was 2d per week.

The Misses Howarth's Private School

This was situated at 83, Hawarden Road in a house named The Hawthorns, which is still there. Miss Francis Blackwell, a teacher at Penyffordd school, left to be married and she later returned as Mrs Howarth in 1895, she retired in 1924. It was her second daughter Miss Howarth who set up this small private school. There were three sisters, one worked in the offices at John Summers, and the other two, Miss Alice and Miss Sarah (who was always called Miss Howarth), were teachers. Two rooms were used, one for the infants, taught by Miss Alice, and the other for the juniors, taught by Miss Howarth.

French lessons began in the infant class, children who went home for dinner played games in the back garden. The entrance examination for Hawarden Grammar School was sat in Penyffordd School. The school closed in 1954.

St. John's School, Penymynydd, 2000.

Penymynydd School football team, 1979.

Meadowslea

The imposing black and white building, (perhaps a reflection of Chester's architecture?), namely Meadowslea has served as a distinct landmark in Penyffordd for over a hundred years and has a very interesting history. In the 1770s Peter Hughes, a yeoman, leased the Fownog tenement from Sir Edward Lloyd. The first mention of Meadowslea is in *Slaters Directory* for 1868, where the building is described as Fownog Hall. The owner, Mr Meadows Frost, was then in residence — his monogram can still be seen on the gateposts at the top of the drive.

The Census of 1871 shows Meadows Frost as the owner of Meadow Lea, living there with his wife, Matilda, his children Meadows Arnold, Eleanor Matilda and Frances Amy. His other son Francis Aylmer is not recorded on this census. At this time property consisted of the house plus a farmhouse and out-buildings, stables, gardens, an orchard, a pond and tennis courts. The household also had servants, Rachel Baldwin (maid and domestic servant) plus three housemaids —Cordelia Jones, Anne Parry and Catherine Parry — and a kitchen maid named Sarah Baines. There were also two grooms, Thomas Bentley and James Clutton.

Meadows was the eldest son of Frances Aylmer Frost and was born in Bridge Place, Chester on 13 May 1819, he had three brothers. The Frost brothers, Sir Thomas Gibbon and Robert, had increased the profile of an already wealthy and influential Chester family by the year 1881. The firm of F. A. Frost & Sons, corn merchants and millers of Steam Mill Street employed over 100 men.

Apprenticed to his father at the Steam Mill, Meadows was said to be very active and dedicated to his work. He would arrive at the Mill before 6 a.m. and on occasion would ride the 24 miles to Ellesmere leaving Chester at 4 a.m. An energetic and enthusiastic young man he would walk a further three miles to the canal in order to supervise the wheat delivery. Later he would attend the corn market and ride back to Chester the same day. In 1844 however, perhaps influenced by his marriage on 25 May to Matilda the daughter of Samuel Berend, a Liverpool business man, he left the family firm and set up on his own account in Liverpool as a cotton merchant. Initially in partnership under the name of Stolterfoth, Frost & Merchant, he eventually continued independently as Meadows Frost and Co.

From the earliest days members of the Frost family had played an active and prominent part in public life and Meadows Frost's father, Francis Aylmer Frost, set him an example serving as a freeman in 1824, a councillor in 1836, and an alderman in both 1844 and 1849.

Meadows was elected a councillor in 1851 and held office as Mayor of Chester* 1858–9 and 1859–60. Although retaining his business in Liverpool, Meadows retained his Chester connection and lived at 6 Little St. John Street. Following his two years as Mayor he was appointed an Alderman in 1863. On retirement from business he came to live at his country home, Meadowslea in Penyffordd in the late 1860s.

Meadows Frost and his family became involved in the public and community life of our area and also the wider area of Flintshire. He became a magistrate in 1879 and accepted appointment as High Sheriff of Flintshire. His son, the Rev. Francis Aylmer Frost, did important church work in the parish of Hope, and was responsible for bringing the mission church to Penyffordd in 1878. After helping his brother-in-law the Rev. John Rowlands of Hope, introduce a branch of the Church of England Temperance Society, Francis began mission work. The dial

* Chester's influence in this area is evident, as maps of the 19th century show that the Mayor of Chester and Chester Corporation owned large pieces of land.

of the clock face of Hope Church is dedicated to the marriage of the Rev. John Rowlands to Miss Florence Frost on 14 September 1880.

There are many references to the Frost family in the old Hope parish magazines, clearly showing their involvement in the community, presiding over fetes and functions, which were often held at their home. Here are just a few examples:

1878 May — Mrs Meadows Frost has most kindly consented to take a stall at the Bazaar, £45 3s. 9d. was raised. £5 donation from his Grace the Duke of Westminster.

1885 — Miss Meadows Frost — gift of bookmarks presented to the church.

1888 17 December Baptism — Lettice Mary, daughter of Francis Aylmer and Emma Louise Frost, of Meadowslea.

The field below the hospital was known as the 'Park' and was used for fete days such as one in 1910 which was led by the Buckley Band. Later there were teas, dancing and cricket matches were also held here. In 1912, the grounds were lent by Mrs Meadows Frost to the Sunday school of the Mission Church, with the permission of H. C. Wrench.

Meadows Frost died in 1883 at the age of 63 years. An account of his death and funeral was documented in the *Chester Chronicle* in great detail:

The funeral took place on Wednesday, and was at the special request of the deceased, strictly private, which explains the non attendance of the magistrates of the city and the corporation of Chester, which through their respective officials requested permission to be present at the obsequies. The cortege left Meadowslea at half past ten, proceeding via the Lache Lane to Chester, arriving at the cemetery at half past one. Through the village of Hope (Penyffordd) and the neighbourhood, the respect in which the deceased was held was shown by the general lowering of blinds. The deceased own carriage contained his two sons, Mr Meadows A. Frost and Mr F. Aylmer Frost, and the Rev John Rowlands, Vicar of Hope, his son-in-law, Sir Thomas Frost was in his own carriage with his two sons, and his brother, Aylmer Frost, Esq. The next carriage was that of Mr Robert Frost, who was accompanied by his two sons. Dr Dobie came in his own carriage. Fifteen very beautiful wreaths and crosses were laid by the family and servants upon the coffins as it was being lowered into the family vault ...

There are gaps in information about later residents of Meadowslea, although it would appear from the indentures that the Frost family retained ownership until the house and grounds were sold in 1913.

We have therefore consulted the census returns in order to discover who lived there and what they did. This has given us some indication of the use of Meadowslea during the sixteen years before it became a hospital.

The census of 1881 shows Frances Aylmer Frost as the owner and he is described as a 'Cotton Merchant'. He had a housekeeper (Maria Rotheram) and a butler (William Owen). Francis married Emma Louisa Russell in 1885. The indentures for 1913 and 1915 refer to a previous indenture of 17 June 1885 which shows that provision had been made for Francis and Emma Frost to live at Meadowslea and it was to be held in trust. Francis Aylmer died on 2 April 1897.

In the census of 1891, a Mrs Margaret Johnston was living at Meadowslea, a widow aged 42 years, with one daughter and two sons. She had seven servants.

The Census of 1901 had some surprises as it revealed Meadowslea to have been a Private Boarding School run by the Headmaster Mr Wilmot C. Pilsbury from Birmingham, who lived with his wife Lucy and sister Marion (who

The original house at Meadowslea,which formed the nucleus of the hospital.

was also an assistant teacher at the school). The boarders were boys of between the ages of seven and ten, and as you can see by the census were from all over the country including one boy from Wyoming in the United States of America. There were also servants. In this census there was also a young girl from America aged sixteen living at Sunnyside, Penyffordd.

At the beginning of the 20th century Meadowslea entered a new era when it became a hospital for the treatment of tuberculosis. The indentures for 1913 and 1915 show that Meadowslea (plus pleasure gardens) were sold by Meadows Arnold Frost (Meadows' son), the Rev. Edward Meadows Russell and Emma Louisa Frost (widow of Francis Aylmer) to the King Edward VII Welsh National Memorial Association for the sum of £1,200, and a further piece of land was sold for £150.

Meadowslea Hospital

The King Edward VII Welsh National Memorial Association was established as a permanent Welsh memorial to the late King, who had died in 1910 and had been a popular throughout Wales. He had taken a keen interest in the plight of the poor and lower classes as well as the National Association for the Prevention of Tuberculosis. A conference was held in Cardiff, with representatives from north and south Wales, including the Lord Mayor of Cardiff and other mayors and dignitaries from Parliament and Councils. Mr David Davies M.P. of Llandinam proposed the establishment of a memorial in the form of a network of hospitals and sanatoriums throughout

Wales for the treatment of tuberculosis. He presented the Plas Llangwyfan Estate to the association, upon which was built the North Wales Sanatorium. As a result of this hospitals such as Meadowslea were established, dramatically changing the role of the house forever.

As the *County Herald* reported on 4 July 1913: 'A pretty residence in Penyffordd has been converted into a Tuberculosis Hospital. A lady Principal has been appointed, and it is in her favour that she is a Welsh Nursing Sister from one of the London Hospitals'.

Meadowslea, the new District Hospital, served both Flintshire and Denbighshire, and was opened for the reception of 19 patients on 14 July 1913. Later, with the addition of two open-air shelters,

The gatehouse at Meadowslea. Note the mongram of the Frost family on the gatepost.

there was an increase to 19 patients (14 male and 7 female). Over the years, as tuberculosis became widespread, the demand for beds increased — in 1923 there were 53 beds and in 1928, 56 beds.

According to written reports the hospital received four types of patients:

1. Cases for diagnoses, presenting special difficulty.
2. Ambulant cases, while suffering from acute exacerbation.
3. Advanced cases who may be returned to work.
4. And Isolation cases who needed efficient nursing care.

The Second Annual Report of the King's Fund, written on 25 July 1914, gives the names of the staff working at Meadowslea: Margaret Davies (Matron), Emily Lawday (Sister) and Ethel Williams (Probationer). A House Committee governed the hospital.

Patients were obliged to stay within the grounds throughout their treatment. They were taught personal hygiene and precautions against the spread of infection. They were discouraged from spitting, which was considered to be a source of infection. The £5 fine imposed for spitting in the street may well have been the result of this belief.

All age groups had to be isolated and it was very difficult for loved ones not to be able to visit, sometimes for months. It was noted in the Area Officer's report that:

*Frost arms
granted 1869*

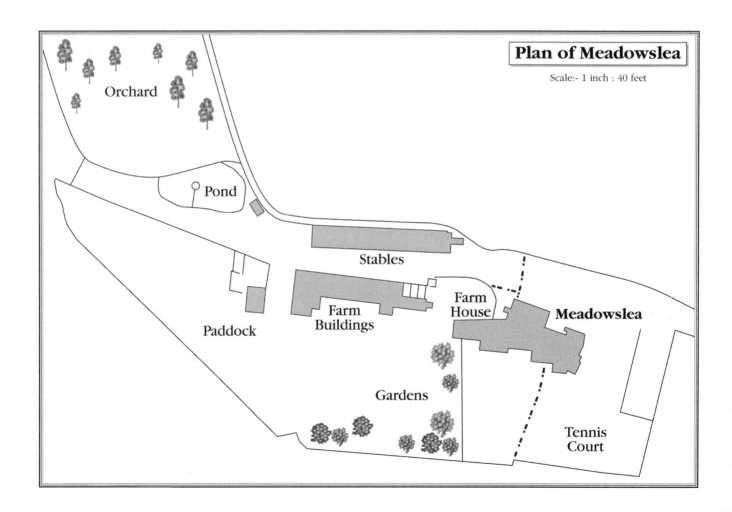

Meadowslea, 1930s, showing the hospital wards built in the grounds of the house.

... comparatively large numbers of patients from Lancashire continue to invade the northern part of this area, most of whom seem to be under the impression that residence in North Wales alone will cure them. Most of them are in a hopeless condition.

This shows the dreadful fear and desperation felt at this time by the victims of tuberculosis.

Care committees were formed in both counties. Their basic function was to help the households who were dealing with tuberculosis. Nursing care also had to be organised and there had to be close co-operation with existing nursing organisations. In March 1913 a conference had been held in London with representatives from the Queen Victoria Institute for nurses, the North and South Wales Nursing Association and Montgomeryshire, with a view to securing nursing services. The Welsh National Memorial Association contributed an annual sum of £5 in respect of each nurse employed. Funds and donations were also given by various nursing associations, such as Connah's Quay £50. The Red Cross and St John's also provided care.

W. E. Hopkins, L.R C.P. (Acting Tuberculosis Physician) complimented the nursing services at Meadowslea in 1915:

> I am especially fortunate in the staff in this area. I am much indebted to the Matron and nurses at Meadowslea Hospital, who conduct this Institution most efficiently ... The Tuberculosis Sister [Kate Parry] for the two counties has the special advantage of knowing the district well, and has rendered excellent service.

The First World War had a direct affect on men who had been treated for TB and been accepted for service in the Army or Navy. The physical and mental strain of war often proved too much for them, and many suffered a complete breakdown. There is a wooden cross in the mortuary, which has the inscription: 'Edmund Arthur Dean, 1st class. Died 21 June 1919. He served in the Royal Navy on HMS *Victory*'.

Dinam House, a nurses' home was built in 1946 and opened by Lady Davies, Sir David Davies's wife. Unfortunately, after performing the opening ceremony she collapsed and died.

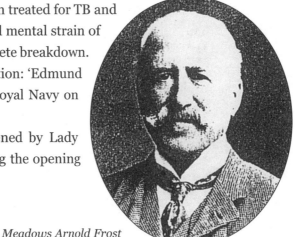

Meadows Arnold Frost

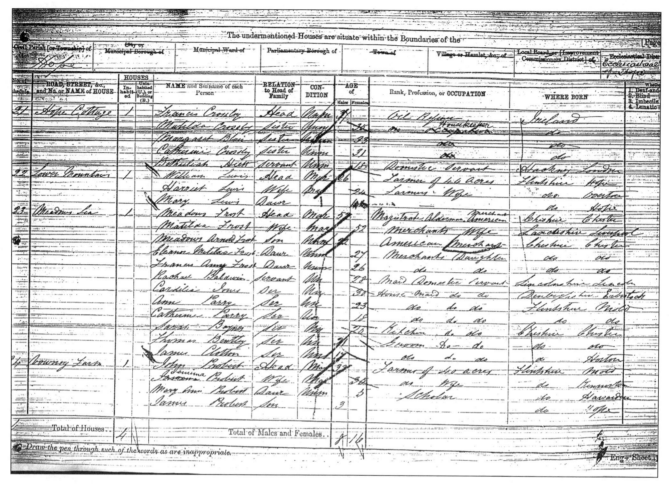

Census return for Meadowslea, 1871.

During the early and mid-decades of the twentieth century many young people died at Meadowslea, and the hospital gained a terrible reputation, which persisted for many years. Consequently many elderly people in the 1960s often refused to be admitted, remembering as they did friends and family who had died there. Penyffordd for many meant literally 'the end of the road'.

New methods of surgery and medical treatment brought hope to those suffering from tuberculosis. Even so patients still had to spend months away from family and friends, fortunately it was recognised that there was a need not only for medical intervention but also for mental and spiritual help in order to overcome the frustrations and monotony of hospital life.

The Christian Fellowship organisation Toc H, was the ideal vehicle to fulfil this aim. It was established in memory of Gilbert Talbot, who was killed in 1915 during the First World War. It was the first welfare centre for soldiers set up in Poperinghe in Belgium. Its headquarters known as Talbot House.

The local branches of Toc H had been helping to relieve the tedium of life at the hospital for some years. In all this work it became evident that there was a lack of suitable facilities to cater for the social and religious life of this community. As

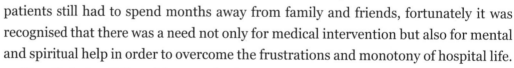

Visiting hours Meadowslea, 1925

Road, Street, &c., and No. or Name of House	Houses			Name and Surname of each Person	Relation to Head of Family	Condition as to Marriage	Age last Birthday (Male / Female)	Profession or Occupation	Employer, Worker, or Own account	If Working at Home	Where Born
Cronog Hill	1			William Cannon	Head	M	44	Coal Miner Foreman	Worker		Cheshire Chester
				Margaret Do	Wife	M	46				Carnarvon Llandden
				Mary G. Do	Daur		16				Flintshire Kinnerton
				Elizabeth Do	Daur		11				Do Hope
				Robert Williams	Boarder	Wid	74	Living on own means			Do Mold
Cronog Hill Sunnyside	1			Amelia H. Hill	Head	Unm	50	Do Do Do			Lancs Ashton under Lyne
				Amelia H. Johnson	Mother	Unm	57				London
				William A. Macfadyen	Adopted Son		7				Lancs Manchester
				Edith Rothwell	Visitor	S	46				Do Do
Cronog Hill Sunnyside	1			Richard Houlgrave	Head	M	56	Retired Blacksmith			Do Rainhill
				Alice Do	Wife	M	53				Do St Helens
				Grace Do	Daur	S	16				United States America
				John N.J. Do	Son		9				Lancs Woolton
Meadowslea	1			Wilmot C. Pilsbury	Head	M	34	Head Master Priv Boarding Sch	Own Acct	At Home	Birmingham
				Lucy Do	Wife	M	32				Lancs Pendleton
				Marian Do	Sister	S	29	Assistant Teacher	Worker		Leicester Leicester
				Henry Baker	Nephew		7				Lancs Levenshulme
				James Morris	Boarder		10				Yorkshire
				Nicholas P.T.E. Shotton	Do		10				United States Wyoming
				Thomas W. Brown	Do		9				London Harringay
				Alan Kinnell	Do		9				Do Sydenham
				Gilbert Do	Do		7				Do Streatham
				Annie Cooper	Serv	S	22	Housemaid Domestic			Hereford StheLacey
				Susannah Turner	Serv	S	17	Cook Dom			Do Collington
				Elizabeth M. M'Lachlan	Visitor	M	42				Kent Charlton
				Leonard B. Stott	Do		9				Lancs Toxteth
Cronog Farm	1			William Taylor	Head	M	57	Farmer	Own Acct	At Home	Cheshire Chester
				Sarah Do	Wife	M	58				
				Edward Jones	Boarder	S	21	Coal Mine Labourer	Worker		Flintshire Hope
Total of Schedules of Houses and of Tenements	5			Total of Males and of Females			18	14			

Census return for Meadowslea, 1901.

patients were treated sometimes for two years or more the need for better facilities was obvious. The Toc H branches of Hope and Caergwrle, Buckley and Mold initiated a project to build a recreation hall and chapel. Other branches in the north Wales area also pledged support. The hall was to be large enough for bed-fast patients to be wheeled there, and a relay system from the hall to the wards conveyed programmes.

The appeal began on June 21 1954, and the site was chosen:

A mixed bag of spade men such as clerks, business men, teachers etc. began with the preliminary task of site clearance and excavation, while others contacted local Toc H branches and other willing volunteers. With the help of a tractor called the Green Linnet and a mechanical shovel the site was ready for foundation work to begin by the end of July. There were a number of craftsmen in this branch also the Clerk of the Works for the County. There were also volunteers from the villages who gave up their time free of charge.

The dedication of the chapel by the Bishop of St. Asaph and the opening of the recreational hall took place a year later on Saturday 25 June 1955.* This was a considerable achievement and a wonderful resource, which still benefits patients today.

* The chapel's four stained glass windows (representing 'The Four Seasons') will be included in the new unit in Wrexham in 2004. The late Mr K. Hugh Dodd, auctioneer rescued them from the Ellesmere (Shropshire) Workhouse when it was demolished before the Second World War, and donated them to Meadowslea Hospital.

Stained glass window showing St. Margaret, Queen of Scotland

As a result of new drugs, treatments and a better understanding of the causes of tuberculosis, it was almost eradicated and so in the early 1960s Meadowslea became a long stay hospital for elderly people. This meant that those who had suffered strokes or other debilitating illnesses which prevented them from returning to their own homes and living independently remained at the hospital, which became their home.

In 1974 there were 72 beds, it was overcrowded and short staffed. However after considerable discussion between management and nursing staff the beds were reduced. This enabled staff not only to improve care but also to improve the environment, and they endeavoured to create a fine balance between hospital and home. The reduction of beds meant that staffing levels improved, enabling posts to be created for occupational therapists and physiotherapists.

During the 1980s and 1990s more resources became available in the community, in the form of nursing and residential homes and community staff, which enabled patients to be discharged with a package of care. A day hospital was established at Talbot House enabling those in the community who needed further medical intervention to come in for the day. Respite care was also provided. Both these services are still being provided.

Weekly services are held in the chapel, for the patients, and Talbot House is the venue of entertainment and the annual staff concerts, which are held at Christmas time and enjoyed by all including the staff!

Voluntary help in the hospital has been provided over the years by various organisations. The Red Cross, the WRVS and the League of Friends. These groups have not only raised funds to buy equipment and comforts for the hospital, but also have provided help such as the shopping trolley and somebody for patients to talk to.

Above: Clearing the site for Talbot House.

Right: The official opening of Talbot House.

Above: Mrs Gwen Lloyd and 'Aunty Ada' at the opening of Talbot House.

Right: One of the stained glass windows in the Chapel.

Above: Meadowslea. Top left: the altar in the hospital chapel.

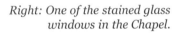

Above: A staff fancy dress party at Meadowslea. Hospital.

Above: A group of nurses and patients at Meadowslea. in the 1950s.

Right: Talbot House and Chapel, Meadowslea.Hospital.

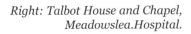

Meadowslea, 2003

Once more Meadowslea faces the challenges of an uncertain future. Two new rehabilitation units are to be built to replace not only Meadowslea, but also Dobshill and Trevalyn Hospitals. This means that our hospital will close in 2004 and this outstanding landmark with such an interesting history could be bulldozed to the ground! A sad end to a hospital which has served this and its surrounding communities so well.

Part Three: Penyffordd and Penymynydd 1890– the present

Shops & Inns

Both villages were very active in the early part of this period and there were many more shops. Maps showing the location of these premises can be found on pages 89 and 97.

Penyffordd

We begin our journey on the Chester to Bala turnpike road, *i.e.* the Corwen (or Rhos) Road.

1. *THE RED LION*

This is the oldest inn in the village. In 1820, when it was known as the Duke of Wellington, it was advertised for sale by Mr Ward. As can be seen by the advert it consisted of 30 acres of land with fine young timber. This area was known as Rhos y brwyner. In the census of 1841 it was detailed as Rhos Tavern, Thomas Jones being the publican and farmer. By the census of 1861 the name Red Lion had been established. The Hughes family were in charge for over 20 years followed by another long-serving publican, Peter Snelsdon. Later licensees were Mrs Mercer and Mrs Hinds.

The Red Lion was located on a busy road and in 1892 it was noted that four beds were available for travellers with stabling for five horses. By 1903, however, this business had declined and the accommodation was described as poor.

2. Mr and Mrs Miller and their son Wilfred kept a grocery and newsagents shop (where the chemist is now). In a room upstairs at the back was a small café, popular with railway travellers. In 1939 a legal document stated: '... they carry on a small general grocery business, their son is drawing no salary and they make just enough to live'. As one resident recalls, Mr Miller did not like children! The shop was taken over by James Griffiths & Son of Buckley.

3. *THE MILLSTONE*

This inn stands on an important junction where the roads from Chester and Hawarden meet. In the 1851 census the landlord was

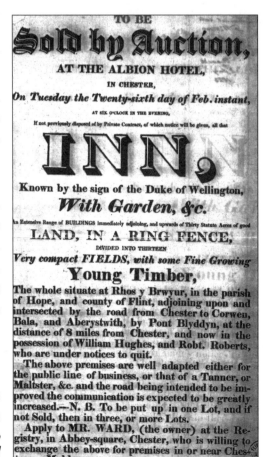

Sale poster for the 'Duke of Wellington' inn, 1820 (which later became the 'Red Lion'. [FRO D/DM/2]

Left: The Millstone Inn in the early 1920s..

Below: the view up Hawarden Road with the Millstone Inn on the right, c.1910.

Below: Inside the Millstone Inn under new management — Mr Jim Bell.

John Williams, who was also a tailor. In 1861 farmer John Bentley was the landlord, followed in 1871 by John Parry. From evidence deduced from maps the Millstone was remodelled between 1871 and 1900. Mr Joe Davies states that his grandfather worked making bricks for the rebuilding. The clay was obtained from a large hole in the field opposite the school. By 1881, George Hollins was the landlord remaining so for at least fourteen years. Business was good and two bedrooms were available for visitors or workmen with stabling for two horses. Social functions, as well as farm sales, were held in the large upstairs room.

The Millstone was owned by a brewery in 1903, Wilderspool of Warrington, who later became Greenhall Whitley Ltd. When Mr Venables was the landlord, candles lit the rooms and beer was poured from jugs. There have been several landlords each making changes to the building and interior. As times changed and the car became a popular mode of transport, Jim Bell made the garden into a car park.

FESTIVAL GARDENS

At this junction was an area known initially as Alley Corner and was a continuation of a public footpath leading from Wood Lane. This piece of land was bought by the people of Penyffordd in 1951 and became known as the Festival Gardens after the famous Festival of Britain. There is now the Millennium Clock on this site and gardens.

4. Drapery and Wool Shop.

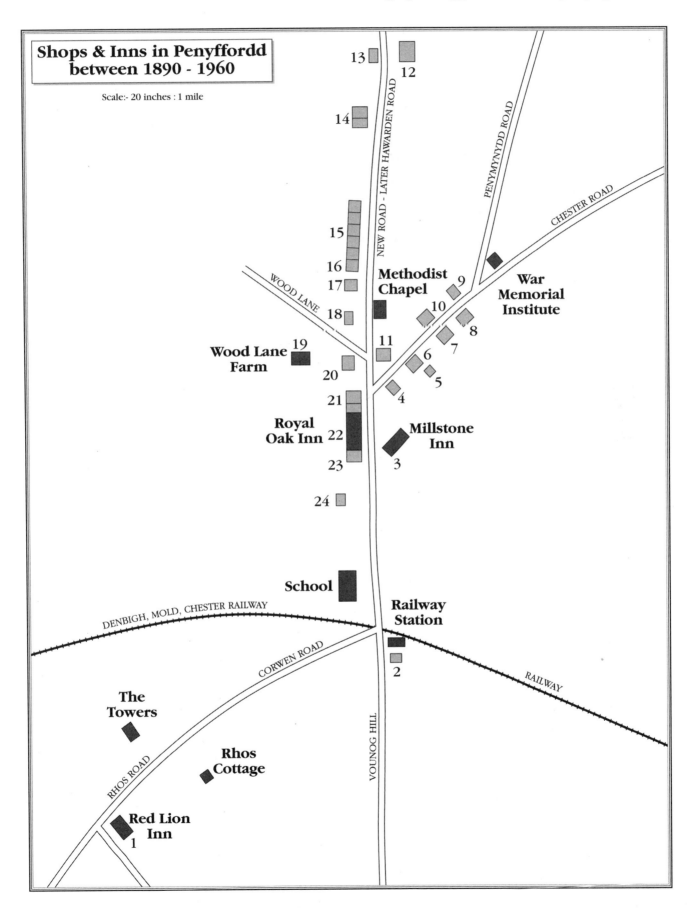

Shops & Inns in Penyffordd between 1890 - 1960

Scale:- 20 inches : 1 mile

13
12
14
NEW ROAD - LATER HAWARDEN ROAD
PENYMYNYDD ROAD
CHESTER ROAD
15
16
17
WOOD LANE
18
Methodist Chapel
9
10
War Memorial Institute
11
Wood Lane Farm   19
20
8
7
6
5
4
21
Royal Oak Inn   22
23
Millstone Inn
3
24
School
Railway Station
DENBIGH, MOLD, CHESTER RAILWAY
CORWEN ROAD
2
RAILWAY
The Towers
VOUNOG HILL
Rhos Cottage
RHOS ROAD
Red Lion Inn
1

Chester Road., c.1920.

5. Small cobblers shop run by an employee of Fred Davies, Penymynydd.

6. Mr Wilcock's Reliance Garage. He sold batteries for the wireless set. Mr C. Ford later took over the business. This was the site for the village's first Co-op store in 1903.

7. When the first chip shop closed, Neddy Edwards opened another one in a small hut.

8. Part of Liverpool House has been a shop for many years. Here was a bespoke tailoring and drapery business run by Mr J. Griffiths. There have been many businesses over the years, including a chemist and greengrocers. It is now the village Post Office.

9. Fish and chip shop opened by Mr John Willie Hibbert when Neddy Edwards's shop was closed and taken down.

10. Griffiths (Grocers) Ltd, when they closed down the vacant premises were taken over by the Royal British Legion.

11. The Post Office. The postmaster was Mr Hughes helped by his daughter Miss Nellie Hughes who later became the village postmistress (she retired in the 1960s). It was also a telegraph office, and telegrams were delivered by bicycle for 6d a time. Proprietary medicines were also sold, a supposed cure for any illness. The building has been demolished and the site is now is a car park. The first Post Office was in Beaconsfield Terrace.

Penyffordd village with the Post Office (centre, facing the camera) 1914.

12. The Co-operative Store. On 15 May 1903 a meeting was arranged in the village to consider the advisability of forming a Co-operative Society, as the time had now arrived when every working man should do the best he could for himself and family. A plot of land was secured on the Chester Road, on which a wooden shop was opened in December 1903. In 1905 the Penyffordd & District Co-operative Society dividend was 1s. 6d. in the £1. Before 1940 a much larger building was built on this new site by the Buckley Co-operative Society and its opening was well remembered as a free box of groceries was given to anyone spending over a certain amount. This is now the site of the Spar shop.

Hawarden Road with Jakeman's Pioneer Garage on the right.

13. This garage was owned by Mr H. Jakeman and was known as the Pioneer Garage. In the 1950s it became a milk bar/café and was described as being full of brass. When the café closed the building reverted back to being a workshop.

14. From 1927, on a Tuesday and Friday morning, No. 61, Hawarden Road, housed the Midland Bank, which later transferred to No. 63. Two male employees would travel by train carrying a briefcase full of money!

15. Mr and Mrs Smiths' grocery store, where locals recall buying two Woodbinc cigarettes and two matches for 1d. This was once part of Beaconsfield Terrace.

16. Here Miss Chesters ran a sweet shop in her front room.

17. This shop had several owners, one of them R. Foulkes who sold children's and women's clothing. Then, in 1933, Miss Lily Tudor took on the business selling sweets, *etc.* When she married Mr Arthur Jackson they named the shop Pandora Stores and expanded the business into a general grocery shop.

Mr & Mrs Albert Smith in the doorway of their grocery shop, 1969.

18. Butcher's shop owned by Mr Skinner, the building was later demolished.

19. The Hewitt family of Wood Lane Farm supplied milk, then later poultry to the village and beyond. Along Wood Lane there was a football field and the cricket pitch. This lane led to Bannel Wood, which was cut down, also to Wood Lane Road which came out close to the Whitewell Farm.

20. Mr. John Griffiths moved his shop from next door to the Royal Oak, almost onto the site of the old Tin Church. He rented his butcher's shop from the Hewitt family. His father Percy Griffiths had set up the old shop.

Right centre: Miss Lilly Tudor inside her sweet shop. Bottom right: Mr Arthur Jackson outside the Pandora general grocery shop.

Griffiths' butcher shop with Percy Griffiths standing in the doorway, 1910.

21. Mr Dolby was the ironmonger and tinsmith. He was a sportsman and wore plus-fours with his gun dog always by his side. Dai Williams took over the business also offering electrical repairs and the delivery of paraffin.

22. *THE ROYAL OAK*

The first recorded publican was William Griffiths in 1861. He supplemented his income by farming. In 1871 Thomas Davies had taken over the inn and 24 years later was still landlord. He and his two sons were also shoemakers and his daughter the barmaid. In 1903, the owners of the Royal Oak were Lassalls & Sherman, brewers of Caergwrle, and the licensee was John Maddocks. Harry Eccleston was a landlord in the early years of the 20th century. Albert Ankers ran the pub for a number of years and would complain if the drinkers got too rowdy and if they stamped their feet too hard as the whitening fell off the cellar ceiling!

Right: The Royal Oak..

Below: The landlord, Mr Ankers (right), and customers of the Royal Oak (Arthur Buckley, Frank Mollington, Freddie Griffiths and one other) pose for a photograph in 1935.

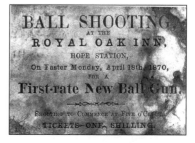

There were two beds available for travellers and a stable for a couple of horses. There was a garden belonging to the Royal Oak at the side of Wood Lane and a bowling green behind it, which was greatly enjoyed in the 1930s.

23. Another branch of Griffith's (Grocers) Ltd. A small van was used to deliver customers orders.

24. This garage was built by Mr E. S. Bellis in 1924. He repaired cars and radios and had an accumulator for charging batteries. During the Second World War petrol rationing meant he had to find work elsewhere. The garage was later bought by Mr C. Ford, who specialised in motor-cycles.

BALL SHOOTING,
AT THE
ROYAL OAK INN,
HOPE STATION,
On Easter Monday, April 18th, 1870,
FOR A
First-rate New Ball Gun.

SHOOTING TO COMMENCE AT FIVE O'CLOCK.
TICKETS—ONE SHILLING.

Advert for a Ball Shooting contest at the Royal Oak in 1870.

Griffiths' grocery shop, next door to the Royal Oak and then Griffiths' butcher shop. The 'Tin Church' can be seen in the distance.

Interesting houses in Penyffordd

RHYD-Y-DEFAID

At this end of Stryt Isa is Rhyd-y-defaid, which consists of four houses with a bridge over Blackbrook stream. This area is mentioned in 1353 as Ryt-y-Devet in a document which records the gift of this piece of land in the township of Hope Owen, to Gronwen ap Grufydd ap Iorwerth ap Meilir also Howel ap Madoc

Hawarden Road Garage, July 1930.

ap Grufydd ap Phelip on 29 June 1353. This was on the drovers' route to and from Bala. The Rhyd house is probably mainly seventeenth century and is timber framed. There was evidence of there being an early, steep thatched roof, which was later covered with corrugated sheeting before restoration. A wicker hood stood over the end fireplace, but it was stolen. Underneath the flagstones was a beaten earth floor, which had never been disturbed.

Placed in the brickwork of the bridge over Blackbrook is a milestone, indicating that Chester is eight miles and Pontblyddin one mile.

HOPEHEY

This stood in Rhos Avenue off the Rhos Road, and is a very old cottage, which was very likely to have also been thatched before recent renovation.

RHOS COTTAGE

The Reverend J. H. K. Ward sold the cottage in 1868 to Mr. Edward Peters of Chester, who was an ironmonger. The cost was £875 and included the Red Lion public house and land. Mrs. Connah lived in Rhos Cottage as a child and she recalls the cellars being full of water! It was a smallholding and her

Bannel Wood at the top of Wood Lane.

Left: Rhos Road in 1914.

Below: Rhos Road in 1936. Postman Henry Ward speaks to Glyn Jones (left), 1914. The Towers garden wall is on the right

family all had to help. She delivered milk locally and churned butter. Poultry were sold at Christmas.

The Mystery of the Penyffordd Stone

Whilst discussing village life with the late Mr Ivor Edwards, I was shown a stone object in his garden. This is a carved stone in the shape of a circular basin (as depicted in the sketch, which also shows the measurements). It appears to have been carved from one piece of limestone and is beautifully made.

After some debate we decided an expert needed to be involved to ascertain the origins of this stone. We contacted Mr Gordon Hill who is an archaeologist, unfortunately he was unable to visit Penyffordd, however from photographic evidence he was able to tell us the following:

The circular shape of the stone bowl suggests that it is ornamental and is not a common sink or wash basin, as these are rectangular. On the other hand it could be used in some form of manufacturing or brewing ... It is possible that it could be a church or monastery item. The age of the stone is uncertain possibly Middle Ages or later.

As this information was based on a photograph only we took Mr Hill's advice and contacted Emma Chaplin, Principle Museums Officer for Flintshire. She saw the stone basin and sent images and information to Steve Grenter at the Wrexham Museum Service, who sent these comments:

I would love to say definitely it is so and so, however, sadly it is one of those objects which could have a variety of uses and be of any date from Roman

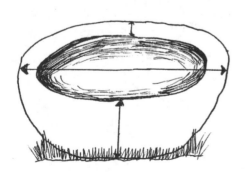

The Penyffordd Stone which measures:53 cms in length, 27 cms in height, with a 7cm rim.

Left: Hope Road.

Below: Hawarden Road.

onwards. I would guess at an agricultural use probably dating to the last two to three hundred years. If the hole goes all the way through [it does] then that might be the way for water to be piped into it. Looks a bit crude for a fountain basin, a bit small for a farm basin.

In order to look for the possible origin and use of this stone, we examined the advertisement for the sale of the Duke Of Wellington in 1820, which is in close proximity, and saw on this a reference to the premises being well adapted for that of a tanner or malster. The location of a monastery in this area is also a possibility, within 2 miles in fact — the Augustinian Priory of St Thomas the Martyr was discovered in Buckley. Mr Derrick Pratt identified the chapel, with a priory which was established by the Augustinian brotherhood during the latter part of the twelfth century.

These are just two of the possibilities which may show the stone's use and origin, and all we are able to produce. Perhaps one day we will discover the truth. Meanwhile we can only say, we do not know.

THE TOWERS

We do not know the early history of The Towers, sometimes known as Penyffordd Hall or Penyffordd House. It was described in the 1850 tithe terrier as a house, buildings and garden owned by Thomas Jones

Above: Hawarden Road, 1935.

Left: Hawarden Road, 1923.

The Towers, Rhos Road.
[S. Cameron]

and tenanted by Thomas Griffiths, who was farming 20 acres. In April 1871 it was said to have had recently erected farm buildings.

By 1891, a solicitor, Hugh Goodman Roberts, was living there with his wife and three servants. In 1892 Mrs Roberts visited Penyffordd School and also sent books and pictures to be used as prizes. The Roberts family was still there in the census of 1901. The house was very imposing with a large square tower, beautiful gardens and an orchard. In 1908 a Miss Bury was living there and she held a small garden party in the grounds.

The next resident in the Towers was Mr Frank Hurlbutt and his sister Mary. Mr Hurlbutt was the second son of Henry Hurlbutt of Queensferry Hall, proprietor of Davison's Brickworks, near Buckley. In 1908 he became a justice of the peace and served as High Sheriff of Flintshire 1918–9. He was an authority on porcelain and not only had an extensive china collection but wrote four books on the subject. He and his sister were very generous donors to the Penyffordd Mission Church, and also gave money to the parish of Hope's War Relief Fund. He left the Towers and went to live at Hartsheath, where he died in 1944. He is also remembered as having the first motor car in Penyffordd.

In 1931, Mrs E. H. Lloyd Vaughan from Ireland sold the house to Miss M. Hyde Sievewright who was rather reclusive. Local residents remember the large tiled hallway, a sedan chair in the tower and bathing as children in the small lake in the garden. Sometime later the house was divided into three flats and the once beautiful gardens neglected. The house was demolished in the 1970s, the trees were cut down and a small estate of houses built on the former grounds.

Penymynydd

1. THE HORSE AND JOCKEY

Our earliest information is taken from the indentures of 1838 detailing a lease agreement between Sir Stephen Richard Glynne, John Bellis and Robert William. In 1848 a mortgage of £49 10s. was raised against the property. In the 1871 census John Bellis was the publican and also a coal miner. In 1879 John Fox of the Castle Hill Brewery in Ewloe, sold the *Horse and Jockey* for £470 to Thomas Bate of the Kelsterton Brewery, Connah's Quay. By 1903 the owner was the Northgate Brewery Company of Chester and its licensee was Annie Ellis. It offered very limited accommodation and closed as a public house

Bill of sale for the Horse & Jockey, Penymynydd, 1879.
[FRO D/BC/3306]

Sold to Thomas Bate Esqr. of Kelsterton in the county of Flint all that freehold licensed Beerhouse known by the name or sign of the "Horse & Jockey" Penymyn in the parish of Hawarden in the county of Flint together with the Shippon, outhouses yards and right of roadway into yards for the sum of four hundred and seventy pounds, and I bind myself to give a good and effectual title thereto, otherwise the said to be null and void. Dated at Kelsterton this 8th day of February 1879 John Bellis.

John Armour – Witness.

around 1950. It is now a private house.

At the crossroads stands Cross Farm, the home of Mr Tom Jones's family since 1899. In the sale catalogue of June 1848 it is described as a new house and buildings. Mr Jones recalls the coal miners squatting by the wall waiting for Bellis's bus to Buckley. After the harvest the corn went to the Tinkersdale Mill, usually about six bags were taken and six bags of flour were returned. Tramps used to sleep in the barn and, as they sometimes smoked, the family were always afraid of fire.

There were many accidents at this cross roads. On 1 October 1911 two cars crashed and both drivers were killed.

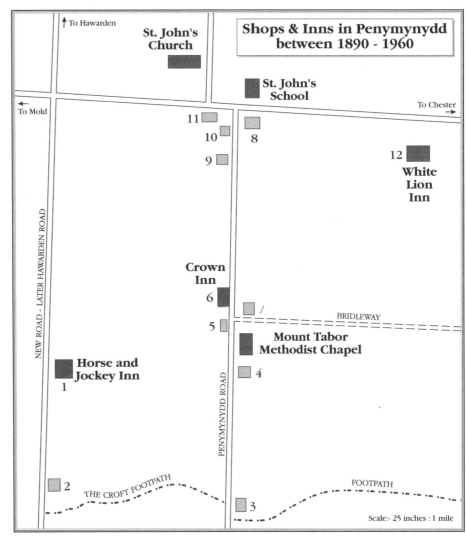

2. Mrs Fox had a confectionery shop and sold sherbet and fizzy pop to cyclists on their way to Hope Mountain and Caergwrle.

3. Miss Roberts sold candles, oil, donkey stones and black lead for grates. Well Farm across the field, was where the family of Mr Joe Davies lived. Here there was a well with steps, which was used by the local community because of its pure water.

4. This was the home of Tom Ellis who delivered green groceries from a horse and cart.

5. Fred Davies made and repaired shoes and clogs and also sold factory made

Cross Farm.

Davies' bootmakers shop, with Mr Fred Davies in the doorway.

shoes. His shop was a popular meeting place for men where subjects of the day were discussed around the stove.

6. *THE CROWN INN*

This was a small inn which offered no guest facilities, just basic drinking. In 1861 James Thomas was the landlord and on 17 July 1873 and he signed an agreement with John Fox of the Castle Hill Brewery in Ewloe to supply ale and porter. The beer from Castle Hill Brewery had a characteristic taste, as very hard water from a spring in Wepre Woods was used in the brewing process. A special strong beer was brewed for Christmas called 'Lambs Wool'. Thomas Jones was the landlord in the 1881 census, followed by Thomas Reynolds (both also worked as coal miners). The Crown Inn was closed by the brewery in 1914.

Below: Manchester House, tailor and drapery store (J. Griffiths) 1900. The Crown Inn is in the background (with two chimneys).

7. A shop in a small hut where sweets and some groceries were sold.

8. John Dean Griffiths grocery shop. This was a very busy shop as customers came from Broughton, the Warren and Dobshill. A resident recalls hams hanging outside the shop.

Below: J. D. Griffiths' shop in Penymynydd, there was also a branch in Penyffordd. Among the staff are A. Jones (Padeswood), W. Powell (Dobshill) and T. Davies (Penymynydd).

Below: The delivery van for Griffiths Grocers Ltd (formerly J. D. Griffiths).

White Lion Inn, Penymynydd.

9. Manchester House, where T. E. Griffiths, tailor and draper, sold underwear, haberdashery, cotton, etc. This business was later run by Mrs Ivy Dodd.

10. A bakery for Griffiths grocery shop opposite.

11. This was stabling for a carrier business. Horses and carts delivered goods to Hawarden, Hope, Doddleston and other villages.

12. *THE WHITE LION*

This was built in early 1846. The census of 1851 records John Jones as publican and farmer of 17 acres. In 1861 William Davies was licensee and 10 years later his widow had taken over running the pub and small farm. By 1903 Mrs M. Jones from Hoole in Chester was the owner and the pub was leased to the West Cheshire Brewery of Birkenhead. As the *White Lion* was located on a busy road from Chester to Mold, accommodation was often required and four beds were available with four or five stalls for horses. As cycling became popular many cyclists clubs called for non-alcoholic drinks for refreshment on Sundays.

By 1920 Thomas Iball was landlord (also a farmer of 11 acres). He had cattle, poultry and pigs on his smallholding. His wife Jane took over as licensee and when she died in 1977, at the age of 99 she was the oldest licensee in Britain. After Jane (Polly) died Brenda and Arthur Jones took over the pub until it closed on 27 October 1992.

Other businesses in Penyffordd and Penymynydd

For a number of years there was a small general store in Alyn Drive. In 1955 it was run by E. Jones.

Down Terrace Lane, Mr Hall and son, then later Mr Driffield, ran a market garden where locals could buy fresh vegetables, especially tomatoes.

Older residents remember the door to door deliveries by horse and cart of green groceries, milk and paraffin, the latter brought round by Mr Huxley. Later bread and cakes were carried by Jack Hurst of Caergwrle riding a motor bike and side car! Later still small vans delivered goods around the area.

Other skilled workers offered essential services to the community. These details are from the census of 1891:

> 6 dressmakers, one of them being Miss E. A. Edwards
> 2 tailors, Samuel Tilston and E. Bellis
> 3 shoemakers
> 1 milliner
> 6 joiners
> 3 blacksmiths. One forge was at Waters Green, Penymynydd where the blacksmith was Thomas Owen, the other forge was on the Pontblyddyn Road.

Wheelwright shop, Lower Mountain Road, 1913. L–R: William Price, William Roberts (wheelwright), H. Eccleston, Joe Roberts, Jack Scott, Bob Martin, Charlie Martin, Johnnie Jonathon. The boy and girl lived in a nearby house.

1 wheelwright, Mr William Roberts. In 1913 his advertisement read: 'William Roberts and son, Wheelwright, shoeing and General Smiths. Funerals economically furnished under personal supervision Est. 1870'.

Coal was brought by rail to the sidings at the Hope and Penyffordd station, where it was unloaded by coal merchant L. E. Lloyd (and later by W. E. Hughes), who advised that 'Best Staffordshire and other coals delivered to all parts of the district'.

In the 1930s Joseph Hewitt of Wood Lane Farm was a motor proprietor who offered a taxi service.

There was a police station next to the Beeches, which moved to the Vounog Hill. In 1891 there was a Police Sergeant in the village and in 1901 a police constable.

It is inevitable that we have not been able to mention every business in the villages. We wanted to give you some understanding of how our communities were thriving and busy. In fact shops and trades provided vital local employment for many, as can be seen in the 1901 census, 26 in Penyffordd and 11 in Penymynydd.

The staff of C. Parry, builder of Penyffordd. Back : Alec Gittins, W. Wright. Front: T. Parsonage, Geoffrey Bartley.

The Development of Housing

The construction of two railways encouraged many people to come to live in the villages, as they made Wrexham, Chester and Deeside within easy reach for employment. An advertisement placed in a local paper in 1904 read as follows: 'Room to let in a popular resort with bracing air and lovely scenery, Preswylfa Hope Station (Penyffordd)'.

Mr Harding built bungalows at the top of the Vounog Hill, and W. Astbury built Vounog Park in the 1930s. The semi-detached houses sold for £435 or £450, with a dining room.

Two areas of council housing were constructed, one along Hawarden Road in the mid-1920s and another in 1948 between Rhos Road and Vounog Hill.

From the 1960s onwards there has been a great deal of housing development in all areas of the villages, either side of Penymynydd Road, farm land belonging to Rhos y brwyner and Wood Lane Farm also adjacent to Abbot's

Lane. In fact, Penymynydd and Penyffordd are now joined by housing. Unfortunately many of the shops have disappeared.

Utilities

Government intervention

In 1842 Edwin Chadwick shocked his contemporaries when his sanitary report demonstrated how much more unhealthy it was to live as a labourer in an industrial town than in any other condition. The results led to legislation in 1847–8, which allowed local authorities to take over existing waterworks and build new ones. Two Acts in 1875 pushed forward the cleaning up of water supplies. In 1854 research in London identified the problems of the environment and its effect on health. This research stated the following recommendations:

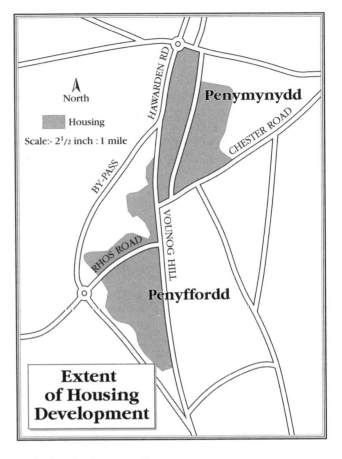

Extent of Housing Development

Good and perfect drainage was essential.

An ample water supply free from contamination by the contents of sewers, cesspools and housedrains.

Habits of personal cleanliness and domestic cleanliness needed to be improved amongst everyone.

Water

The provision of water to our villages had been under discussion since 1889. Mr W. Bellis 1899, who was the Sanitary inspector for the area, reported:

Water supply throughout the district generally good. Saltney water from Chester Water works. Kinnerton not satisfactory-obtained from open water course and shallow wells and cannot be at all times free from pollution.

The main sources of water in both Penyffordd and Penymynydd were the wells which can be seen by an examination of 1875 Ordnance Survey map.

There were many wells in Penyffordd, almost every house and farm having their own private water supply. Some of these wells are still remembered, such as the one located outside the Red Lion, where there was also a huge oak tree and a pen for sheep. Another well was to be found at the Red Houses just past the old village school. This well had a shallow glazed earthenware slopstone for doing the washing. Mr Alec Astbury remembers the wriggly things coming out in the water — hence a filter was used!

Penymynydd on the other hand did not have as many wells; there was the Silver Well and also Well House Farm. Many, however, relied on their supply from Whitewell, which also served the Spon Green area of Buckley. This latter well is still visible from the road, standing in the Dale Fields with an iron fence around it.

According to Thomas Cropper, in his book *Buckley and District* (p.106), at times of drought, which was a serious and common occurrence during a long spell of dry weather, people would remain at the well throughout the night waiting patiently for their turn. Big tin cans and plenty of work for tinkers was the order of the day. One person who lived near Spon Green was a familiar figure with a large 50–100 gallon barrel drawn by a donkey, selling 1d cans of water procured usually from the Whitewell, Penymynydd. Water from this well was also transported to Granny Fox's shop, where she would make fizzy pop which was bought by local children and cyclists from Liverpool who were on their way to Hope Mountain or Caergwrle.

It was recognised therefore, that there was a need for a reliable safe water supply but it took some considerable time for it to be provided. A letter in the local newspaper, dated 28 August 1907, written by Charles Phillips, argued that it was unfair to give the village of Penyffordd water and not to do the same for other districts in the parish of Hope Parish. Another report, 30 March 1906, describes a petition calling for mains water supplies to be laid to both Penyffordd and Penymynydd. The Wrexham & East Denbigh Water Company were prepared to introduce a scheme even though the land had not yet been built on. The Council however wished to detach our two villages from this scheme because many of our houses had wells which they considered to be adequate and less expensive.

It was argued, however, that a reliable source of water was required especially as there had been an outbreak of typhoid fever in the area which, according to the doctors, was caused by contaminated wells. Every well cost £30 whereas it would cost £3 to provide water for each house. In October 1908 work on bringing piped water to the village was reported to 'be in progress'. The water rates in 1927 were £1 2s. 3d. During the Second World War, when farms were in need of water, the Land Army girls used water divining. One particular girl, Barbara Littler, was said to be particularly gifted in this art.

Housing and Sanitation

During William Gladstone's government, the Public Health Act of 1875 obliged authorities to install drainage and sewerage. Obviously these projects would cost money and so there was some reluctance to do so in each village.

Housing conditions were unbelievably bad in the mid-nineteenth century. Some houses were poorly built, damp and unsafe. Rooms had no light and were unventilated. Others were overcrowded and so were condemned. A report on one such house in Penyffordd stated:

> The house 'Rhosbryn' is an isolated house, consisting of one living room and one bedroom on the ground floor, 4 small windows only one opens; the bedroom floor is damp, it is neither boarded nor tiled; one of the gables is in a dangerous state and might fall at any time. There is a no closet accommodation or drains. The roof is thatched and badly in need of repair.

The matter was reported to the council. Notices were ordered to be issued and it became unoccupied.

The Nuisance Removal Act of 1846 instigated the appointment of the first Medical Officers of Health. Reports of notifiable diseases such as measles, diphtheria and scarlet fever (which were sometimes fatal) were sent to the Medical Officer of Health. Fever cases were sent at this time to the Cheshire and Wrexham Infirmaries. The two Medical Officers of Health, Mr Thomas Moffatt and Mr William Roberts were paid £25 and £10 per annum respectively.

In 1873 the Inspector of Nuisances was Mr Dashwood Parry who was paid £50 per annum. The Inspector gave the owners of cottages in Penyffordd, Penymynydd and Stryt Isa fourteen days to put right the problems of sanitation in their cottages. Here are a few examples:

Edward Thornton owner Penymynydd; The pig sty's belonging to 3 cottages in the occupation of himself and others are in too close proximity to cottage in the vicinity-to be rectified in 14 days.

George Hughes one of the owners. To provide privy accommodation and drainage, the pigsties are too close to the cottage mentioned ... to be rectified in 14 days.

To the managers of St John's National School. To remove privies which are in a bad state further from the school.

There were approximately thirty cottages mentioned in his report on Penymynydd.

Penyffordd and Stryt Isa also had problems mainly with drains and privies. Hope Station was mentioned three times regarding its drainage and privies.

18 February 1876 — House in the occupation of Thomas Griffiths, Rhyd y defaid, Hope; Mrs Jane Williams and Mrs Hamner owners: I visited these premises, the houses are thatched and the roof is in a dilapidated condition, consequently does not keep out the rain ... It consists of two rooms, kitchen and bedroom, both small, each having a window, very small, which does not open. There is a pig sty next to the house but at present no pig.

11

Appendix C.

SUMMARY of Sanitary Work done in the Rural Sanitary Districts of Hawarden Union.

		1898.	1899.
(1.) INSPECTIONS.—	.. .. ..	451	577
(2.) NUISANCES ABATED.—			
Drains cleaned and repaired	.. ..	18	16
Drains reconstructed	.. .. ..	29	31
Drains trapped	.. .. ..	34	44
Waste pipes disconnected	.. .. ..	6	3
Waste pipes provided	.. ..	..	8
Cesspools abolished	.. .. ..	1	1
Privies and ashpits repaired and covered	..	19	43
New privies and ashpits provided	.. ..	18	36
Ashpits cleansed	.. ..	21	35
Offensive accumulations removed	.. ..	6	8
Houses cleansed and limewashed	.. ..	7	8
Yards paved	.. ..	..	11
Roofs and eaves troughs repaired	.. ..	5	9
Overcrowding	.. .. ..	..	5
Animals improperly kept	.. .. ..	..	12
Houses disinhabited	.. .. ..	..	5
Houses made fit for habitation	.. ..	..	3
(3.) ACTION TAKEN RE ABATEMENT OF NUISANCES.			
Letters written	.. ..		108
Informal notices issued	. .. .		42
Legal notices issued	.. ..		31
Prosecutions	.. ..		4
Orders granted	.. ..		3
(4.) WATER SUPPLY.—			
New houses supplied and certificates granted		90	75
Old houses supplied	.. .. ..	79	15
Samples taken for analysis	.. ..	5	7
Samples condemned as unfit	.. ..	3	4

Summary of sanitary work carried out in the rural district of Hawarden Union. [FRO]

It is interesting to note the number of pigs kept by householders particularly in Penymynydd.

Electricity

Electric cables were laid in May 1928 in Penyffordd, Vounog Hill and Rhos Road. Tenders were invited for the provision of electric lighting of the Institute the contract being given, on 19 October 1928, to E. S. Bellis who had provided the cheapest. The installation was completed on 11 January 1929.

Communication

Public telephones in Chester and north Wales were introduced by the Lancashire & Cheshire Telephonic Exchange Co. Ltd. in the late 1880s with the opening of an exchange in Chester. Flint also had an exchange but this was closed by 1897. All the separate telephone companies in the UK were absorbed by the National Telephone Company by the mid 1890s. In 1921 there was a party line which ran from Buckley to Kinnerton with ten subscribers on it. Eight of these were from Penyffordd:

1X2 — A. S. Sandbach, corn merchant. Penyffordd.

1X3 — J. J. Rowlands, farmer, Model Farm, Penyffordd.

1X5 — J. D. Griffiths, grocer and baker, Penyffordd.

1Y1 — S. Done, farmer, Terrace Farm, Penyffordd.

1Y2 — Hall Bros., nurserymen and tomato growers, Penyffordd.

1Y3 — A. Griffiths, grocer, Penyffordd.

1Y4 - R. C. Wrench, farmer, Penyffordd.

1Y5 — A. Peters, Platt Farm, Penyffordd.

The effects of two World Wars

The Great War, 1914–18

For many people the events of 1914 marked a decisive turning point in their lives, after which the world was never to appear the same again. When the First World War broke out in August of that year everyone thought it would be over by Christmas, certainly local newspapers gave this impression. This was understandable as, since the 1850s the wars fought in Europe, had tended to be of short duration.

There were many reasons given why men joined the Colours. There was a certain amount of patriotism, but for many there was a sense of adventure and an escape from everyday life which sometimes included unemployment. However, the loss of life of so many young men touched both their families and the community. The war affected not only the way people lived but also after 1914 women were to become more active in different occupations.

Recruitment

There seems to have been a great deal of pressure put on our men to enlist in the armed forces. Recruitment meetings were held at the Penyffordd Council School. These included a lantern show which showed several of the Caergwrle contingent's joining the Colours, as well as images of warships, aeroplanes and King George V and Queen Mary. Strong appeals were made to the young men present to join one of the infantry or cavalry regiments. Patriotic songs were sung, one such by Miss May Roberts who sang 'It's a long way to Tipperary'. Another recruitment drive included a Mold contingent of the 5th Reserve Battalion, Royal Welsh Fusiliers,* who paraded in the district. This was considered to be a good muster with the majority of men in khaki and some in plain clothes. It had the desired effect of recruiting several men from Penyffordd, Penymynydd and Caergwrle. Blue Cards were also considered as a form of recruitment and the district was divided into sections with the canvassers, mostly women, being appointed to call upon young men of military age whose name appeared on the card.

Those men and boys who were either too old or too young for war joined the Volunteer Training Corps. This was originally an unofficial group having neither uniforms nor rifles. They were to the First World War what the Home Guard was to the Second World War. According to local newspapers the Penyffordd Corps was one of the

---

* The name Royal Welsh Fusliers was not officially changed to Royal Welch Fusiliers until 1920.

first, if not *the* first to be established in Flintshire, belonging to the Flintshire Battalion. The object pf the V.T.C. being to train men for the defence of the country against invasion. There were regular marches to various venues such as Hawarden and Kinnerton, and they were drilled twice weekly under the instruction of a sergeant major. On one of the marches to Hawarden they were accompanied by a Sergeant Major Coote. Thirty to forty members were present, and on arrival they went through their drill exercise in the presence of the Lord Lieutenant of the County of Flint, Mr Henry N. Gladstone. They were highly complimented on their smart appearance and excellent manner, as a result the formation of a group at Hawarden was discussed.

Rifle shooting was practiced at Mold Drill Hall and at Connah's Quay, there was also a shooting range for musketry (rifle) practice a short distance from the village on the Chester Road. We believe this could have been down Barracks Lane, where we have also been told horses from the Cheshire Yeomanry Cavalry were stabled.

At a rally for local men held in Mold the following comment appeared in the newspaper: 'The men presented a smart appearance with bowler hats and brassards and formed one of the best companies on parade'. Officers and men carrying out special duties of a temporary nature wore armlets or brassards, usually with lettering denoting their work. There were also monthly church parades to the Primitive Methodist Chapel, St. John's Church and also to Zion Presbyterian church. The Corps had by now decided to purchase uniform for every member who had put in twenty drills. Mr Hurlbutt, J.P., of Penyffordd House, rendered valuable financial assistance and new uniforms were received in December 1915.

Roll of Honour and Casualties of the Great War

Casualties as we can see by the Roll of Honour in the Memorial Institute and the churches were many. Amongst those who lost their lives or were wounded or decorated were:

Private *Alfred Hemmings* (241473) 5th Bn. Royal Welsh Fusiliers was killed in action in Palestine on Monday 26 March, 1917, aged 20. He was the son of William and Mary Hemmings of The Cottage, Penyffordd and had been employed as an apprentice tailor with Mr Thomas E. Griffiths. He has no known grave but his name is recorded on the Jerusalem Memorial, Israel (Panels 20–22).

Private *John William Roberts* (6025) 5th Bn. The Connaught Rangers, was killed in action in Palestine on Sunday 10 March 1918, aged 34. He was the son of Joseph Roberts of Laburnum Cottage, Penymynydd and the late Martha Roberts. He is buried in Ramleh War Cemetery, Israel (U.57).

The local press records that Mr and Mrs Rowlands of The Barracks lost their third son but, sadly, does not name him. Neither he nor his two brothers appear on the local war memorial.

Lance Corporal *Bennett William Fallows* (345089) 24th Bn. (Denbighshire Yeomanry) Royal Welsh Fusiliers, was killed in action in Belgium on Saturday 7 September 1918, aged 24. He was the son of Bennett William and Elizabeth Fellows of Well House Farm, Hartsheath. He has no known grave and his name is recorded on the Ploegsteert Memorial, Comines-Warneton, Belgium (Panel 5).

J. Stormer was badly wounded in France, he had worked on the railway and was very popular.

Frank Griffiths died on active service. He may have been Gunner Frank Griffiths (67129) B Battery, 83rd Brigade, Royal Field Artillery, who died in France on Thursday 21 March 1918 and who has no known grave. His name is recorded on the Pozieres Memorial, Somme (Panel 7–10).

Private *Samuel Wilcock* (21495) 10th Bn. Royal Welsh Fusiliers, was killed in France on Wednesday 16 August 1916 during the battle of the Somme, aged 27 years. He has no known grave and his name is ecorded on the Thiepval Memorial, Somme (Pier and Face 4A). He had joined the RWF fifteen months previously and was shot whilst rescuing a wounded comrade. He left a widow and two children.

Private *Arthur Griffiths* (119399) 9th Bn. Royal Welsh Fusiliers, of Rhos Cottage, died of his wounds in Flanders on Thursday 20 September 1917. He is buried at Oxford Road Cemetery, Ieper (III.A.7), Belgium. He joined up even though, as a coal miner, he was in a reserved occupation. He was described as cheerful and amiable.

Richard Lewis died on active service.

Lance Corporal *Henry T. Asbury* (262808) Syren Forces, Royal Engineers, died in Russia on Saturday 1 February 1919, aged 36. He was part of the Allied force sent to the Murmansk area in support of the White Russian forces in their war against the Bolsheviks. Born in Penymynydd, he was the son of Richard and Emma Asbury and the husband of Mary Elizabeth Asbury of Belle Vue Terrace, Penyffordd. He is buried in Murmansk New British Cemetery, Russian Federation (B.8).

Charles Jones died on active service.

Lance Corporal *J. Percival Messham* (21494) 16th Bn. Royal Welsh Fusliers, was killed in action on Wednesday 23 August 1916 during the battle of Ypres. He is buried at Essex Farm Cemetery, Ieper, Belgium, (Grave II*i.e.*6).

Arthur Griffiths died on active service.

Sergeant *Thomas Davies*, Royal Army Medical Corps, the son of Mr Ithel and Mrs Rose Davies of Penyffordd, gained the Military Medal. His brother, Gunner *George Vincent Davies* (831931), A Battery 241 Brigade, Royal Field Artillery, was killed in action in Flanders on Tuesday 11 September 1917, aged 21. He is buried in Vlamertinghe New Military Cemetery, Ieper (XI.H.7). Another brother was discharged from the army as medically unfit and two other brothers also served during the war.

Miss Howard of Penyffordd had been a nurse in the war and gained the highest nursing award. She died in 1942.

In the *Hope Parish Magazine* it was reported in 1918 that:

A number of soldiers have been on leave, Stanley Parker is now gazetted a 2nd Lieutenant in the Royal Welsh Fusiliers. Sergeant Jos Gerard, Bert Williams, Jimmy Bell and Harold Jakeman were over shortly before Christmas, all looking well. William Edwards and Frank Griffiths were over from hospital but have now been able to rejoin.

When leave was granted it was very short, in fact some soldiers from Australia spent their leave on farms in north Wales.

Certain jobs such as colliers and farmers, were exempt from military service however they contributed 3d per week out of their wages (boys 1d per week) towards the war effort.

During this conflict women became very involved in the war effort in the community, supporting the men serving at the Front. The villages seem to have become a closer-knit community during the war as everybody fought for the same cause. Subscriptions to 'War Relief Funds' were donated and collected and some women worked on the farms, some being given training at Plas Newydd farm in order to become efficient at agricultural work.

In August 1914 a Voluntary Aid Association was set up in order to make suitable garments for wounded soldiers and sailors. The Penyffordd and Penymynydd Sewing Club sent the following articles to a depôt in Mold for despatch to the Royal Welsh Fusiliers in the Dardanelles in 1915: 47 Shirts, 4 prs mittens, 26 prs of socks, 14 mufflers. This was but one example of many such articles provided by the villagers and dispatched over the war years.

Eggs were also collected for wounded soldiers. During the year January 1915–January 1916 a total of 9,270 eggs (including 2,955 sent by St. Johns, Pentrobin and Hope and district) were distributed as follows for wounded soldiers:

St John's VAD Hospital Chester	1,725
Red Cross Hospital Chester	3,539
Royal Infirmary Chester	2,239
Leeswood Hall	577
Local sick soldiers	290

In the Hope parish magazine of 1916 children from the Council School knitted seven pairs of socks and a number of cuffs and mittens for the 10th Bn. Royal Welsh Fusiliers. The recipients wrote to each of the scholars thanking them saying how much they appreciated their work. In December 1918 there is a note that: 'Friends and supporters of the Sewing meeting will be glad to know that a letter of Good Wishes for Christmas and the New Year and a Postal Order for 5s has been sent to each man serving from this district'.

A family of Belgian refugees stayed in the village for nine months.

Meadowslea Hospital had been opened in 1913 for the treatment of tuberculosis and also for patients with other chest problems. It was recognised however that those men who had been treated for tuberculosis and then been accepted for active service in the army or navy were too weak to take the physical and mental strain of war and many suffered a complete breakdown. The physician considered it best that they were not accepted for military service. A poignant reminder is a wooden cross in the mortuary which is inscribed: 'Edmund Arthur Dean, Stoker 1st Class, who died on 21 June 1919, he had served on the HMS *Victory* with the Royal Navy, and is buried in Hawarden'.

An X-ray machine was presented to the hospital in 1923 for the benefit of ex-servicemen resident in north Wales.

The government was asked to provide a minimum grant of £1 10s. per week for disabled soldiers or to widows of soldiers killed in action plus 5s. for each child. This was paid through the Post Office and not by charity.

Monthly concerts were also held to aid funds.

At the end of this dreadful war a celebration was arranged at the Council School and a knife and fork tea plus plenty of cigarettes were provided for the local heroes.

In 1918 Penyffordd had decided that a village institute was the most fitting memorial to those who had fallen in the war. Colonel Sir I. Vesey, Chief Staff Officer of the Western Command, opened the Penyffordd and Penymynydd Memorial Institute in July 1923. He also unveiled a white marble tablet which was inscribed with those who had fallen in the Great War of 1914–18.

The years between these two wars will be remembered by many. One of the major concerns was unemployment during the 1920s and 1930s, resulting in the miners strike of 1921 and the General Strike of 1926. Many industries in the area were affected making poverty very real.

The Representation of People Act of 1918 widened the franchise to nearly all men and extended the vote to women over 30. It was not until 1928 however that women had the same voting rights as men.

The Second World War, 1939–45

This war was very different from the Great War. There was not the same recruitment drive as lessons had been learned. Technology had made great advances and whereas fighting had always taken place on the mainland of Europe, this war was brought to the doorstep in the guise of aeroplanes which dropped bombs. As before, there were also many fronts to this war, not only in Europe but Africa, Burma and the Pacific.

Many of our men served in these countries, fighting in the North African desert under the command of Montgomery against Rommel, in the 8th Army (the Desert Rats). Others in the Royal Engineers, the Royal Welch Fusiliers and many other regiments, served up to four years on the battlefront. There were also those who served as prisoners of war in Germany or in south-east Asia, having been captured perhaps at Dunkirk or Singapore, who spent many desperate years in the camps. Most of them were reluctant to tell their families of the trauma they had undergone at the hands of our enemies, often suffering nightmares for many years afterwards.

Perhaps even now families do not realise how brave their fathers and grandfathers have been, their medals being kept out of sight. When these brave men returned after the war they found it difficult to adjust to normal everyday life having been away from their families for such long periods.

Amongst those from the area who made the ultimate sacrifice were:

James Bradshaw, died on active service.

Robert Davies, died on active service.

Driver *Thomas Edwards* (T/106732230) Royal Army Service Corps, was killed in action in Libya on Saturday 29 May 1943, aged 21. He was the son of William H. Edwards and Sarah E. Edwards of Penyffordd. He is buried in Tripoli War Cemetery, Libya (6.H.2).

James Ellis died on active service. He may have been Sergeant James Ellis (1052736) of 550 Squadron, Royal Air Force Volunteer Reserve, who was killed in action on Wednesday 3 May 1944, aged 36, flying from RAF North Killingholme in a Lancaster bomber. He was the son of Thomas and Elizabeth Ellis and the husband of Noreen Bessie Ellis of Buckley. He is buried in Cheviers Churchyard, Marne, France (Military Plot, Row 1, Grave 1).

Leading Aircraftsman *Thomas Peter Raymond Hulley* (1411108), 2749 Squadron, Royal Air Force Volunteer Reserve, who died on Monday 22 March 1943, aged 21. He was the son of Thomas and Emma Hulley of Dobshill and is buried in the cemetery of the Church of St John the Baptist, Penymynydd.

Harold Johnson, died on active service.

Joseph Price, died on active service. He may be Fusilier Joseph Price (4203978) 2nd Bn. Royal Welch Fusiliers, who died on 5 May 1942. He was the son of William Evan and Mary Price and is buried in Diego Suarez War Cemetery, Madagascar.

Joseph E. Reynolds, who lived at Warren, died on active service. He may have been Private Joseph Edward Reynolds (1808364) 3rd Bn. The Monmouthshire Regiment, who died on Thursday 17 August 1944, aged 23. He was the son of Joseph and Maggie Reynolds of Wrexham. He is buried in Bannevill-la-Campagne War Cemetery, Calvados, Normandy (XV.C.21).

Sergeant Pilot *John C. Willis* (1621067), Royal Air Force Volunteer Reserve, who died on Wednesday 8 March 1944, aged 26. He was the son of Charles and Ada M. Willis of Penyffordd. He is buried in Tripoli War Cemetery, Libya (7.C.26).

Flight Sergeant *George Harold Williams* (964465), Royal Air Force Volunteer Reserve, who died on Thursday 30 November 1944, aged 26. He was the son of Thomas Harold and Clara Alice Williams and the husband of Joyce Mabel Williams of Penyffordd. He is buried in the cemetery of Christ Church, Ponblyddyn (Row K, grave 22).

Gunner *William Wright* (4201802) 20th Anti-tank Regiment, Royal Artillery. He died on Thursday 20 July 1944, aged 29. He was the son of Edward and Ellen Wright, Penyffordd. He is buried at La Delivrande War Cemetery, Calvados, Normandy. (IX.H.2).

Pilot Officer *Charles Norman Wright* (174338), a navigator in 630 Squadron, Royal Air Force Volunteer Reserve, was killed on 8 July 1944 flying in a Lancaster bomber out of RAF East Kirby. The son of Joseph and Maud Eliza Wright and the husband of Phyllis Collier Wright of Dobshill, he is buried in Omerville Communal Cemetery, Val d'Oise, France (Collective grave 2).

Men who were in reserved occupations such as farmers, aircraft workers, ship builders and colliers volunteered to join the Air Raid Precaution services which included the Auxiliary Fire Service, the National Fire Brigade Service and the Air Raid Wardens. The Air Raid Precaution Act of 1937 forced local authorities to protect and make provision for the public in the event of war. As we have seen by watching TV's *Dad's Army*, the Air Raid wardens often had problems with the public. One such incident was reported in the local newspaper.

On being told that a light could be seen from a bedroom window, whilst the Air Raid warning was in force a munitions worker shouted down to the local PC, 'What about it; Hitler would not bomb a bum place like this, or the bum people in it, and if he did it would cause a bit of excitement'.

There were many who served on a fire watch rota and they remember the essential equipment used, the stirrup

*A group of women war workers employed at the Vickers airaft factory at Hawarden during the Second World War.
[Airbus UK Ltd]*

Interior view of the Hawarden aircraft factory showing two production lines manufacturing Avro Lancaster four-engined bombers. Many of the parts were actually made elsewhere and brought to Hawarden for final assembly. [FRO]

A stirrup pump which was an essential piece of equipment for anyone on firewatching duties during the war. [FRO]

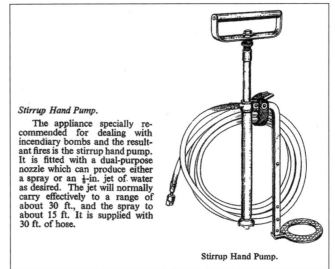

Stirrup Hand Pump.

The appliance specially recommended for dealing with incendiary bombs and the resultant fires is the stirrup hand pump. It is fitted with a dual-purpose nozzle which can produce either a spray or an ⅛-in. jet of water as desired. The jet will normally carry effectively to a range of about 30 ft., and the spray to about 15 ft. It is supplied with 30 ft. of hose.

Stirrup Hand Pump.

handpump and two or more two–three gallon buckets of water, also their tin hats. Fire watch at the Exchange Station meant 3s. a night for volunteers. The cellar under Penymynydd Chapel was used by the firewatchers as was St. John's School.

The Flintshire Constabulary issued secret information to the ARP and other authorities in the county, throughout the war. One such document, issued in 1940, describes action to be taken in the event of bombs dropping and being found:

The enemy have been dropping small HE anti-personal bombs about 3 in. diameter and 4in. long. If any of these bombs should be found, a sandbag enclosure should be built around it. The enclosure should be formed of three tiers each of four sandbags. Care must be taken not to touch the bomb.

Many meetings took place in the Institute where they discussed blackout procedures and plans in the event of an air raid. Penymynydd School had lectures on anti-gas and other ARP lectures, including an ambulance class. The Institute in Penyffordd was taken over by the Air Ministry in 1941. As much as 30s. fine could be imposed for leaving a light on during the black-out. Careless talk, *i.e.* telling someone about shipping movements, realised a £5 fine plus £7 7s. costs!

The Women's Voluntary Service (W.V.S.) was formed in 1938 and were largely responsible for organising Feeding and Rest centres in this area for those who suffered the effects of air raids, perhaps being made homeless. Some of their other jobs included:

Make sure the blackout regulations were complied with.

Arrange heating and boiling water.

Summoning voluntary helpers to assist the police and air raid wardens.

Supplying plenty of blankets, utensils, crockery, etc. in the event of people losing their homes in a bombing raid.

Informing the local council who might need billeting, especially if they could not return home because of unexploded bombs.

Summoning medical help.

The general welfare of the people — provision of emergency meals and a clean centre for temporary accommodation.

Maintaining fire- fighting equipment at the local centre.

The feeding centres consisted of mobile canteens that ensured emergency food supplies were always available *e.g.* tinned meat, tea, sugar, jam, biscuits, tinned milk and Oxo.

Foodstuffs which were received by the County Organiser from the American Red Cross consisted of:

Tinned milk 15,360 tins
Sugar 5,200*lbs*,
Chocolate (cocoa) 1,400*lbs*
Soup 3,800*lbs*

Rice 2,475*lbs*
Cereal wheat 7,300*lbs*
Wheaten flour 5,800*lbs*

BUCKLEY URBAN DISTRICT COUNCIL.

AIR RAID PRECAUTIONS.
ENROLMENT FORM.

Name in Full.. Age............

Private Address ....

....

Business Address ....

....

Profession   Whether single
or Occupation....................   or Married......................
                              Phone Number.......... ....

Please indicate for which of the
following Services you desire to
volunteer. and if for more than one
specify your choice in a named order:—

(a) Auxiliary fire Services
(b) Fire Brigade Reserve   1.................. . ...
(c) Air Raid Warden
(d) First Aid Party
(e) First Aid Post Staff
(f) Rescue Party   2................... ....
(g) Decontamination Party
(h) Ambulance Driver or Attendant
(i) Report Centre Staff
(j) Clerical Work   3.................. .   ...
(k) Storekeeper
(l) Messenger

Are you willing to undergo the
necessary training to qualify you for
the duties which you will be required
to perform in the event of an emergency
arising?

State number of hours weekly you   ....
could devote to training and the hours
at which you could attend?   ....

Have you had any previous training in

[a] Anti-gas Measures   [a]...........................

[b] First Aid   [b].............................

[c] Fire Brigade   [c]...........................

Are you able and qualified to Drive
a Motor Car?   ....

Are you able to provide a Motor
vehicle (if necessary)   ....

If so, state type.   ....

Signed.., ...

Date.......................... 1938

This Form, when completed, should be detached and returned to the
Clerk to the Buckley Urban District Council Offices, Buckley.

E.C. P.9.

An ARP enrolment form for Buckley Urban District Council. showing the variety of war services provided by the local community. [FRO]

Rationing had begun in January 1940 and had a profound effect on the eating habits of the nation. The weekly allowance was:

> 4ozs of bacon or ham
> 4ozs butter (later reduced to 2ozs)
> 12ozs sugar
> Sweets were also rationed

Women were conscripted into industry working at Shotton steel works and the Vickers Armstrong aircraft factory in Broughton where the first Wellington bomber was completed in August 1939. Some women worked at the Royal Ordnance Factory Rhydymwyn, making munitions, others on the railways and buses. They worked alongside men replacing those who had gone to war.

The Women's Land Army in Flintshire was actually formed before the war on 1 June 1939. In December there were ten landgirls, however by 1943 the number had risen to 602. These were volunteers from all walks of life, not only from Flintshire but from Yorkshire and Lancashire. The mother of Mrs K. Edwards **of** Roseneath was in the Land Army and worked on Willis' farm, whilst others worked on Lloyd's farm. Mrs Gwyneth Nesbitt was also a landgirl, joining when she was 17 years old in 1943. For the first six months she worked in Pest Control, which meant killing rats. This was vital work as we had to grow our own food. The rats were either caught in iron traps or chased by a terrier dog into their hole where they were gassed whilst someone stood by the bolt hole and killed them with sticks. In Flintshire there was a Pest Control group of four who killed vermin. Between February 1941 and April 1942 they destroyed 3,545 rabbits, 7,689 rats and 1,901 moles which were skinned and sold for 1s. Rats tails were sold to the government for 1d. each. Not surprisingly Mrs Nesbitt did not enjoy this work and so quickly learned to drive. She also worked on farms and in the fields. The Land Army's jobs were many and varied from milking cows, harvesting and haymaking, even water divining. Their uniform consisted of a brown slouch hat, greatcoat, cream aertex shirts, one green pullover, one pair of brown corduroy breeches, two pairs of dungarees, one overall coat, six pairs of stockings and darning wool, one heavy pair of shoes, gum boots and oil skins. Headscarves and turbans were standard wear for work in the fields.

To save coupons and overcome shortages, arm slings were bought from the chemist at 2s. 6d., dyed and utilised as turbans. There was no official way to wear the uniform, as was noted in the local papers — 'No one can do more extraordinary things with a uniform than a Land Army girl who has put her mind to it'.

In late 1940 and early 1941 the Luftwaffe began to appear over Flintshire. Their main targets were the cities of Liverpool and Manchester. It is thought that in reality most of the bombs dropped in north Wales were the result of poor navigation which meant that the pilots had missed their targets, or perhaps had decided to get rid of the bombs before returning home. Bombs were widely scattered during the four nights commencing on 29 August. Some were dropped on and around the village, however it does not appear that anyone was killed or hurt.

Two high explosive bombs (HE) were dropped on the Rhyd y defaid farm fields on 1 September. Three HE bombs landed in the Padeswood district on the Mold to Chester railway line, which was blocked as a result. When bombing raids were imminent the trains would shelter under the nearest bridge so that the planes could not see the sparks from the engine. These trains carried coal from the local mines and also munitions from the factory in Rhydymwyn. On the 18 November, three HE bombs were dropped on Cold Chimneys, Stryt Isa, destroying five poultry sheds, and two further HE bombs and a container of about thirty incendiary bombs were dropped in Stryt Isa. There were high explosives dropped in a field at Bank Farm, Chester Road, and also on the road by Berwyn cottages, Hawarden Road.

Kinnerton had anti-aircraft guns (Ack-ack) which when used meant shells fell near to the Tin Church in Penyffordd. A Lysander (T1453) army co-operation aeroplane from No 13 Squadron crashed in Silver Wood on 18 November 1940, killing the pilot, Scotsman P/O David Michael Agnew who is buried in Hooton churchyard.

Excitement, not fear, seemed to be reflected in children's memories of the war. Those who were at school had a routine exercise when the air raid warning was given. When war first broke out they were taken to shelter under the trees near to The Towers House, however, their routine changed: one whistle meant hiding under the desk, two whistles meant go into schoolyard, three whistles meant run home to take shelter there (under the stairs or table). An air raid shelter was later built.

Penyffordd School was also involved in the war effort in various ways such as National Savings and Salvage collection, as can be seen by Mr R. L. Parry's report of February 1944 which recorded: National Savings average per child £2 12s. 2d. and paper salvaged since July 1943 amounted to approximately 1½ tons.

There were also gardening plots at Penyffordd. As part of the Dig for Victory campaign 'greens' were planted in the summer and leeks were grown in order to supplement the children's family with extra vegetables.

Evacuees from Birkenhead and Liverpool stayed with local families and went to school with the village children, and appeared to have been accepted. The Zion Chapel schoolroom had an evacuee family from Liverpool living there. Figures show that Flintshire received a total of 19,400 evacuees.

Local children watched convoys of American tanks and lorries driving down the Rhos Road, chocolate and chewing gum from the American soldiers were received with delight. There were also soldiers in tents on Hope Mountain, all these activities were probably for training purposes.

There were Italian and German prisoners of war in this area who were put to work on local farms.

After the war were many changes. Women, who had been out to work in industry such as Vickers Armstrong, the aircraft factory and the munitions factories, were no longer be satisfied with staying at home. The men who had been away had to rebuild relationships with their wives, children and family, many of whom did not understand the dreadful experiences their husbands or fathers had gone through. It was certainly a challenging time for everyone.

The War Memorial Institute

In the *Flintshire Observer* of July 1923, there is a description of the opening of the new War Memorial Institute in Penyffordd:

> An impressive ceremony was witnessed at Penyffordd today week, when an Institute, erected in honour of the men of Penyffordd and Penymynydd, was opened by Col. Sir I. Vesey, Chief Staff Officer of the Western Command. A silver plated key was used to open the door.

The first proposal to build an Institute was mooted in 1906. However on 28 November 1918 there was a meeting to discuss the building of a War Memorial: 'We are all agreed that we should and will do all in our power to honour the dead and benefit those who came back to us'.

Mr James Collinge of Kinnerton Lodge gave about one acre of land between Chester Road and Penymynydd Road. Money was also raised by public subscription. The five Trustees were: William Astbury, builder; John J. Rowlands, Model Farm; Robert Wrench, Blackbrook Farm; Charles Willis, Nant Farm; Jonathan Price Griffiths, Hope Villa. The cost of the building was £1,400, with £500 being donated from the Miners Welfare Fund. The Lord Lieutenant of the County, H. N. Gladstone laid the foundation stone on December 16, 1922.

The Institute consisted of a large airy concert room tastefully decorated in blue and white. At one side, the east side of the hall, was a kitchen and on the other side, a billiard room containing a new table. In the concert hall a piano was provided. Hot water heating was installed. On the opening day, Thursday, 19 July 1923, Colonel Vesey also unveiled a white marble tablet on which is the following inscription:

1914   1918

THIS BUILDING AND TABLET WERE ERECTED

IN MEMORY OF THE MEN OF THIS DISTRICT

WHO FELL IN THE GREAT WAR

Richard Lewis	G. Vincent
J. Percival Messham	Henry T. Astbury
Samuel Wilcock	Arthur Griffiths
J. William Roberts	Frank Griffiths
Alfred Hemmings	Charles Jones.

"Lest we forget"

Captain R. Allen, J.P., Deputy Lieutenant of the County, presided over the opening ceremony in the unavoidable absence of the Lord Lieutenant. There was a large attendance and tea cost 1s. followed by a concert in the evening also costing 1s.

A summer fête was organised for every July at the Institute starting in 1924 and has continued to take place there except for the war years 1940–45. At various times other venues have been Meadowslea on the field known as The Park and also Rhewl Farm.

The use of the hall in the Institute was questioned by those who felt it was primarily a memorial to those men who had fallen in the war. There was much debate about this in the local newspapers, as feelings ran high. There was a letter to the editor of the *Liverpool Daily Post* in December 1923 from a non-committee man, objecting to

Penyffordd War Memorial Institute, c.1925.

the Institute being used for dances less than six months after opening: 'The War Memorial is a sacred memory, if used like this the tablet should be removed where it can be kept with more reverence'. There were other letters, one to the 'old fogey on the council', signed 'broadminded':

Before this Memorial took a tangible form it was promised that it would be a hall for the benefit of everyone locally without exception or distinction. Why then is dancing regarded with such contempt? May I also point out that a large contribution was made by whist drives and dances. I suggest that sooner the better 'Fogies' are replaced by broadminded men, including some service men. On behalf of the dancers of Penyffordd.

This dispute was resolved over the years as other facilities and clubs were developed such as, badminton, a football team, tennis courts and a bowling green. In 1923 a literary committee was formed to discuss operetta and choral ventures. It was not until January 1929 that electric lighting was installed by E. S. Bellis.

In 1930, for the first time, a Rose Queen was included in the Fête, the first being Miss Hilda Roberts. Also in this year the play *Peg O'My Heart* was performed on 16 & 17 December, to much acclaim. Competitive meetings were arranged for the development of intellectual and social interests in the district.

The Second World War meant many changes. The windows had to be darkened to comply with the blackout of the ARP's regulations. There were also lectures held here by the ARP. Land was let as allotments to help with the war effort — at 5s. per allotment. The WVS held whist drives in order to pay for Christmas presents for local men who were serving in the Forces. In February 1941 the Institute was taken over by the Air Ministry.

After the War, in October 1949, a service and ceremony and dedication took place as the second memorial tablet to those local men who died in the war was unveiled.

1939   1945

THIS TABLET WAS ERECTED IN MEMORY OF

THE MEN OF THIS DISTRICT

WHO FELL IN THE SECOND WORLD WAR

James Bradshaw	Joseph Price
Robert Davies	Joseph E. Reynolds
Thomas Edwards	John C. Willis
James Ellis	George Williams
Raymond Hulley	William Wright
Harold Johnson	Charles Wright

"Lest we forget"

The first 'Queen Elizabeth' and her court walk through Penyffordd during the Coronation Pagent of 1953.

In 1951 the Rose Queen was re-established at the annual Fête, the first being Marie Cuckson (née Fox). In the Coronation year of 1953 a pageant depicting Old England and Queen Elizabeth I, was organised, by Mrs Hastie.

The Memorial Institute has been constantly modernised with improvements to the windows, heating, kitchen and decoration, and is still a very important focal point of the village being used for social functions and other charitable meetings.

It is worth remembering the origin of this memorial however, and how important it was to those families of the men who gave their lives in two World Wars.

Entertainment and sport in the late nineteenth and early twentieth centuries

Music and sport played a valuable role in the villages, helping to bring our community together, and also included the wider community such as Hope and Buckley.

Music

Music has always been an important part of village entertainment, there being a Musical Society from the late nineteenth century. The earliest information we discovered of a musical event, was a programme advertising Musical Entertainment, to be followed by a Comic Operetta. As you can see from the programme on page 64, this was held on Tuesday, 1 February 1887, at the Board School.

The Penyffordd United Musical Society arranged many socials which included dancing, singing and games. They held a grand concert on 25 January 1907. The chair was taken by Mr William Huxley. The choir under the leadership of Mr John Brooks sang splendidly. The programme was as follows:

Pianoforte solo 'Lurline' Miss Clemens (Penyffordd)
Part Song 'Comrades Song of Hope' The Penyffordd United Choir
Song 'When Jack and I were Children' Miss Jennie Jones
Song 'My Sweetheart when a Boy' Mr Walter Davies (Chester)
Part Song 'The Village Blacksmith' The Penyffordd United Choir
Song 'The Gift' Miss Alice Chatham

There were many other songs by soloists and the Choir. The evening was finished with *God Save The King*. This perhaps gives you a flavour of activities in the days before television.

A special meeting was held on the 30 September 1930 to set up a competitive meeting to be held, not only to help continue the funding of the Penyffordd and Penymynydd War Memorial Institute, but primarily to develop intellectual and social interest in the district. Present at this meeting were Messrs J. P. Griffiths, Howell Jones and Mesdames Griffiths, Greatorex and Platt. The minutes show the prizes to be awarded for literature and music including: a children's choir action song (age 12–16), essays, recitation, violin solo, pianoforté, best drawing, best specimen of woodwork, best pair of men's hand knitted socks, needlework, impromptu speech, sight reading (piece without stops). The prizes ranged from £2 2s. to 2s. 6d., the total outlay of money being £9 19s. 6d. This new venture first took place 4 April 1931, with people from Wrexham and Mold competing against our villages. The annual competition, now just for children, still survives in the village and takes place in November.

The Penyffordd Girls Choir

Music still is an integral part of village life and the Penyffordd Girls Choir carries on a great tradition. The choir was formed in 1974 and has been very successful. The girls have taken part in many competitions including the Llangollen International Eisteddfod. They have also been on the radio and television. The choir has a very wide repertoire including classical and modern works, folksongs and religious works.

Penyffordd Girls' Choir, 1986.

Drama

Amateur dramatics was enjoyed by many, the Penyffordd Amateur Players put on a performance of *Peg O' My Heart* in December 1930, an inspired performance, according to the local newspaper. The Penyffordd Players drama group was run by Mr and Mrs Hastie of Tanglan Cottage. Mr Hastie was the producer and their three children were also involved. A popular production was Nöel Coward's *Blythe Spirit*.

Later Mr Graham Stanton established the 64 Drama Group. Many villagers took part, not only as actors but also as essential back stage workers. The productions were very popular and there were large audiences in the Memorial Institute where the plays were staged. Some of the productions went on tour to local villages, Leeswood and Pontblyddyn. *Fumed Oak* by Nöel Coward, produced by Hilary Eccleston, won the Flintshire Drama Festival. When the 64 Drama Group finished Mrs M. Gaught set up the Cambrian Opera Group.

Horticulture

The Hope Horticultural Society was also another form of interest which was well supported locally at this time.

The cast of the Zion Church production Zurika the Gipsy Maid, *1936. Performed on 16 March in Zion Chapel School Room.*

The Penyffordd Players.

Playbill for the dramatic production of Noel Coward's Fumed Oak, *the winning entry at the 1966 Flintshire Drama festival.*

Below:Cambrian Opera Group; the cast of My Fair Lady.

" Fumed Oak "

by

NOEL COWARD

CAST *(in order of appearance)*

HENRY GOW	DOUGLAS FAIRCLOUGH
DORIS (His Wife)	BERYL KNAPPER
ELSIE (His Daughter) ...	LIZ ROBERTS
MRS. ROCKETT	
(His Mothe aw)	RENE STANTON

Play Produced by:

HILARY ECCLESTON

Stage Managers	....	David Wilcock
		Ken Hopwood
Lighting and Effects	....	Roy Smith
Decor and Props	....	June Fairclough
		Vera Smith
Make Up	... .	Jean Brown

There will be a 15 minutes interval between plays.

The Fête

The annual fête includes the crowning of the Rose Queen and many other events. This was a day of festivity in the villages with the parade usually led by a band and a local boys movement, sports for the youngsters, and a baby show. These took place after the First World War at various locations, Meadowslea Park, Rhewl Farm and the Memorial Institute. The fête is still held annually, however it has changed, the procession is not quite as big and the fair is now part of the scene. Refreshments are still available, which include hot dogs and ice cream. The baby show no longer takes place.

One of the highlights of the year remembered by many of our local villagers was the picnic at the White Steps, which took place every Good Friday. Bottles of water and sandwiches were the usual refreshments after the long walk. No one seems to know when this started but it was certainly a happy and memorable occasion. The White Steps are still to be found close to the old railway line near Wat's Dyke.

Sport

Sport was enjoyed by many, and there was certainly a variety, which would suit most tastes. Football, cricket, bowls, billiards and tennis were all taken very seriously.

The development of football in our villages has been difficult to trace. We know that both schools, St John the Baptist Voluntary Aided Primary School and Penyffordd Council School, had teams in the early 1920s. They played friendly matches against each other and also travelled to Buckley, Connah's Quay and Broughton schools. There was a football pitch in Wood Lane and in Penymynydd Road. In later years the game was played in Abbot's Lane.

The photograph of the 1947 team shows older boys, however, we were unable to find out who they were. In the late 1950s and 1960s there was team called Penyffordd Villa and at some time during this period there was a 5-a-side team in both villages.

During the early 1970s, there was a move to form football teams for the under-12 and under-14 year old boys of the villages; Edwina and Stan Davies, the late John Rowlands, Geoff Davies, the late Dave Owen and Mike Myers being the founder members. They began by organising a junior football club which played friendly matches to begin with, until a Penyffordd League was formed. Their first strip consisted of their own shorts and the old blue and white shirts of Crystal Palace! They played on a field in Penymynydd Road.

Penyffordd Youth Club F.C., 1947. The team was re-started in 1973, as Penyffordd Villa.

Penyffordd & Penymynydd Youth football team, 1970s.

Left: Rose Queen Dolly Tudor with her retainers, outside Rhewl Farm, 1931.

Below: 1934 Rose Queen Glenys Aston with flower girls Kathleen Bellis and Margaret Griffiths. The car driver is Cliff Parry.

Above: The 'Royal Float', with the 1951 Rose Queen Marie Fox and her Court.

Above: Members of the Caergwrle Boys Brigade passing the old school during the fêt in the 1950s.

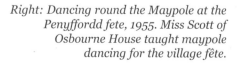

Above: Rose Queen Gillian Edwards and her retainers at the 1958 fete.

Right: Dancing round the Maypole at the Penyffordd fete, 1955. Miss Scott of Osbourne House taught maypole dancing for the village fête.

Right: The Blue Bords dance troupe . Back: Sylvia Sides, Mary Crofts, Sheila Davies, Marion Pugh, Marrie Fox, Ann Millington, Ann Lloyd, Josie Lloyd. Front: Barbara –?–, Beryl Parry, Barbara Parry, Marjorie Jones, Margaret Garston, Josie Pugh. The mascot is Cynthia Rogers.

Below left: The Red Cross tent at the 1957 Fete. Mrs Lloyd, Mrs Hollins, Ms Dolly Davies, Mrs Dora Jones.

Ladies of the Labour Club dressed up as The Girls of St. Trinians entry in the Fete.

Football is still extremely popular, and there is now a Clwyd League, in which both villages play, catering for boys aged between 5 and 17.

There was a bowling green behind the Royal Oak. Many bowling competitions took place here, one example being the Penyffordd Institute vs Buckley Rose & Thistle on 3 July 1926, at Penyffordd. The visitors, being the most experienced set of players, had little difficulty in defeating the newly formed Institute team. A return match was arranged to take place at Buckley. Other bowling events took place on the green at the Institute during the early part of the twentieth century. The committee in 1928 arranged monthly bowling competitions during the summer. The *Chester Chronicle* in 1932 reported the close of a successful season, the best experienced at the Institute Bowling Green. Credit was given to Mr E. Roper, also mentioning veteran Mr S. Lewis, who was 83 years old and partially blind, but did not miss one game.

There are now two bowling greens. The Penyffordd and Penymynydd Community Bowling Club, is situated on land beside the Abbot's Lane Infant School. This was conveyed to the community in 1979 and officially opened in 1980 by Councillor Brenda Davies. It is very popular with all age groups especially those who have retired. Both open and club competitions are organised. The Millstone Bowling Club at the side of The Millstone Public House was laid out at a cost of £7,000.

Cricket was very popular, and a cricket club was formed around 1876. We can show the fixtures arranged for the Penyffordd team in 1904 and 1908 and are sure that some people who will be recognised by name or photograph. The games were played on the cricket field adjacent to Wood Lane and also on The Park at Meadowslea. One such game was reported in the local newspaper in June 1914 before the outbreak of the First World War:

Penyffordd Under-12 football team, 1969.

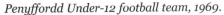

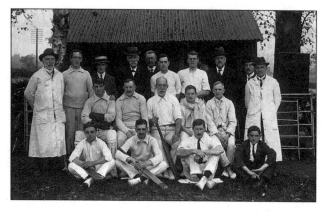

Penyffordd 1st XI, 1919.

A fête was held at Meadowslea. Buckley band marched to the park and dancing, games etc. took place. Particular interest was centred on the cricket match between the ladies and gents; Penyffordd Cricket Club versus a number of ladies. Broom handles were used by members of the club whilst the ladies used conventional cricket bats. The club scored 62 for 7 wickets and the ladies 61 all out. Miss Probert of Hope batted well, there were a large number of spectators.

The matches often had to stop for visitors to the hospital to pass on the public footpath, they had arrived by rail from various destinations. The cricket team was supplied with ice cream from John Willie Hibbert's chip shop!

There were tennis courts at the back of the Memorial Institute and also in the grounds of Meadowslea, however the the Hope and Penyffordd Tennis Club in Park Lane, was formed in 1908, and the courts were laid out on land given by Mr E. R. Randles. Trustees manage it and a committee organises the running of the club.

Initially there were two grass courts, then a third grass court was established by renting adjacent land for £3 3s. per annum, with an option to buy for £100. Later the surfaces of the courts were covered in hardwearing shale. Yet another improvement in 1992 was the all weather playing surface laid at a cost of £33,000.

The fortunes of the Tennis Club have been mixed. It survived two world wars but went through difficult periods in the 1940s and 1960s when membership dwindled. This excerpt is from a very pessimistic letter written by Mr W. R. Parry (Secretary and Treasurer) to encourage support:

S. Bellis, 1932

Owing to varying factors, such as the 5 day week, television and motor cars, the appeal of tennis seems to have lessened and this year we are making a final appeal to keep the club going, for they are facilities worth preserving.

With new and enthusiastic members, interest was revived and the club teams were successful in competitions in the Flintshire League. Ever since 1908, however, at the express wish of Mr Randles, Sunday play was not permitted. In 1963 after consultation with the late donor's children and local residents it was agreed at an extraordinary meeting that playing tennis on Sunday would be allowed.

Opening of the new pavilion at Penyffordd, 1954, by Mr H. G. Northcott, watched by Mr J. Blease, Mr Cliff Parry, Mr Ron Parry (tennis strip), Mrs Kilvert and others.

Two conditions were set: there was to be no play before 2 p.m. and then only for members over sixteen years.

In 1954 a new pavilion was opened by Mr H. G. Northcott. This building has been a source of concern for many years and now, in 2003, club members are raising funds to build not only a replacement but also to install floodlights, which would mean the game of tennis will continue to be enjoyed by many for years to come.

The Millstone Inn darts team.

Village organisations

At the end of the nineteenth century and beginning of the twentieth century there were several organisations linked to the churches.

The British and Foreign Bible Society, 1903, was an association formed initially in 1819. It was a forum to discuss and exchange information for missionary societies. The founding societies were the Baptist, Church, London and Wesleyan Methodist missionary societies.

The Good Templar Lodge (Sisters of the Lodge) Hope and Penyffordd were also active at this time holding concerts in the Council School.

The North Wales Women's Temperance Union 1879–1921.

The Loyal Order of Ancient Shepherds, this was founded in 1826 and was a sick and burial club.

Lastly the Good Templars, belonging to Zion. This was a Temperance Christian Order of the Knights Templar, Scotland.

Members of the Penyffordd Ladies Temperance Club gather on the tennis court at The Towers, c.1900. [FRO 48/12]

Right: Members of the Penyffordd Womens' Institute gather outside the War Memorial Institute in the 1920s for a hyacinth growing competition.

Below: Members of the Womens Institute.

Right: W. I. 75th Anniversary photograph of the local branch, January 1999, Glenys Walker President.

Later in the 20th century we now have other organisations which are still active.

The Women's Institute is a non-sectarian and non-political organisation formed in Britain in 1914. In January 1924 the first meeting of the Penyffordd, Penymynydd and Dobshill Women's Institute was held in the War Memorial Institute, presided over by Mrs Butterworth. Since its formation over the years our local W.I. has offered women the chance to learn new skills, to work collectively for the good of the village and nation, to make new friends and to enjoy themselves. During the Second World War a leaflet put out by the government stated that 'we must remember in wartime that there will be no food to waste, but with care and co-operation we shall have enough'. Our W. I. realised it could play a pivotal role to help women through this difficult period. Classes were given on canning, jam-making, and how to stretch limited food rations. Rose hips were collected to be sent away to be made into vitamin C-rich syrup. They were shown how to re-use old clothes, and of course scarves, gloves and socks were knitted to be sent to those on active service. Through resolutions voted on at the National AGM the movement offered the government a recognisable body of opinion in the country and has influenced decision-makers locally and nationally. Social, medical and environmental issues have all been raised and discussions on Resolutions Night have been stimulating. Our W. I. members have been successful in craft and drama competitions in north Wales. The movement has its own adult education college near Oxford and many local women have taken the opportunity to study a subject of their choice from a wide ranging prospectus. Throughout the years the W. I. has played an important role in the lives of the village women. As Mrs Beavan said at the 1989 A.G.M.: 'There is a greater need now more than ever for an organisation that proves stability'.

Members of the Womens Voluntary Service (later Womens Royal Voluntary Service) which was founded in 1938. Back row: Mrs Roberts, Mrs Rowlands, Mrs Bellis, Mrs Matthews, Mrs Egerton. Front row: Mrs Morris, Mrs Connah, Mrs Lloyd, Mrs Lewis. These ladies helped at Meadowslea Hospital and delivered 'Meals on Wheels'.

The Royal British Legion is a national organisation for ex-servicemen and women, founded in 1921. It provides aid with housing and employment and runs homes for the sick and aged. It also has a role in helping servicemen and women return to civilian life. In 1954, a group of villagers meeting in the kitchen of John Willie Hibbert's chip shop had the idea of building a Royal British Legion branch premises in Penyffordd. Further meetings were held in the Memorial Institute until there came an opportunity in 1958 to buy premises. These belonged to Griffiths (Grocers) Ltd. who had ceased trading. The enthusiasts, with the help of Border Breweries of Wrexham, bought the premises. The brewery gave them an interest free loan and also installed a small bar. The building was enlarged in the 1970s but, as membership grew, it became evident that better premises were required. A decision was made to rebuild on the site, and the new building opened in 1976. The Royal British Legion is a very popular venue for many social functions, including darts tournaments, country dancing and even dominoes.

The Boy Scouts (now called simply The Scouts) were officially set up in March 1965 and the first leaders were G. Butler and John Griffiths (the village butcher). Until they found their own premises they met in a building at Wood Lane Farm. They then renovated the old village school canteen and it opened in 1976 as the venue for meetings. The Scouts offered local boys moral leadership, friendship and a chance to participate in a wide range of sporting activities.

The Girl Guides (now The Guides) started in 1955 and hold their meetings in the Memorial Institute. Their aims are to give service, keep fit with a variety of sport activities (such as swimming, rounders and ice skating). They also enjoy the outdoors, annual camping trips and hiking. They also have to earn interest badges.

The 1st Penyffordd Brownies started in 1954 and the Brown Owl was Mrs Beryl Griffiths. The 2nd Penyffordd Brownies started in 1968 with Brown Owl Mrs P. Smith. The Brownies meet in the Memorial Institute and enjoy different activities, learning new skills, and participate in sports, drama and games.

There are many charitable organisations in which the villagers are involved such as cancer charities and N.S.P.C.C.. There is also an Environmental Group, Flower Club and Wine Club, all of which serve the community and make our two villages work closer together.

Crime

The Kinnerton Sheep Stealing Case

This story is related in a local newspaper, 18 April 1885, and it must be said that the written description of this case is so colourful that it is worth reading for yourselves as it stands. It is the story of a sheep that was stolen from a field in Higher Kinnerton, owned by Mr Jas. Collinge, at Christmas time in 1884. It was traced eventually to the Crown Inn, Penymynydd. The police went to the house of Joseph Millington, however he had run away, and evaded the officers and made good his escape. Nothing more was heard about him until a month later, when it was found that he was working in Blantyre, Scotland, under the name of Price.

The Lanarkshire police were communicated with, the prisoner was apprehended, and he was brought to Mold. The case was fully heard on the 9th inst, before Mr Bankes, when the first witness called was Mr F. Jones, bailiff to Mr F. Collinge, who said he counted eighty-seven sheep in Crompton Hall Park on the 20th of December. On Sunday morning he found one sheep missing, and after a long search he found there were traces of the sheep being taken over a wire fence, and then across some fields and along old roads in the direction of Penymynydd, and to a point opposite the cellar of the house where the prisoner lived. When he had traced the sheep a long distance and finding that it had been stolen, he sent for the police, and he was joined by A. S. Armor and P.C. Langdon who were with him when they reached the house of the prisoner. The police went into the house, then came out and asked him to get a horse and trap to go to Mold to get a search warrant, as he started, the police calling to him again saying the sheep had been found.

He went to the house and to the cellar where he found some sheep entrails, and the marks of blood covered with sawdust. At the bottom of the garden there were many more sheep entrails. The police then brought a whole side of a sheep, and a forequarter, with the shoulder and part of the neck taken from it. It had been recently killed as far as he could judge. The mutton was taken away to Mr Collinge's, and then shown to Mr Lazarus Roberts, the butcher of Caergwrle. The sheep was valued at £4. P.C. George Langdon said he accompanied the last witness and Sergt. Armor to the house of the prisoner at Penymynydd. They went to the house where they saw the prisoner's wife who called her husband downstairs. He came down in about five minutes, when Armor asked whether he could search the house. The prisoner said, 'No, not without the riot act. What is missing?' Witness replied that a sheep had been lost from Mr Collinge's and traced to his house. Prisoner said, 'A sheep indeed, there is no sheep here -if you accuse me of stealing a sheep I'll make it hot for you. ' Armor said, 'If you are an honest man you will let me search your house, if not, Langdon shall remain here and I'll go for a warrant'. Armor and witness then went outside, and in about two minutes the prisoner's wife came out and said something, which caused Armor and himself to return to the house. He went upstairs, and on a bed in one of the rooms he found half a sheep, and a forequarter, minus the shoulder, all being partly covered with bedclothes. He carried it downstairs and gave it to Mr Jones, while they searched the other parts of the house, finding part of the entrails in the cellar. On coming from the bedroom he went to seek for the prisoner, and did not find him anywhere. He asked the wife for the prisoner, and she said he had gone. He did not see Millington again till Tuesday last, at Hamilton, in Scotland. On reading the warrant over to the prisoner, he cautioned him, to which he said, 'I thought to come and give myself up, as it is others that brought me into it. It has troubled me ever since, as I have always been in dread of someone coming for me.' In the train, as they came from Mold, the prisoner said, 'What do you think I will get for this. I expect I shall get five years.' The prisoner inte'rupted the witness at this point and said, "It was only a joke I was passing with you.' Mr Lazarus Roberts, butcher, Caergwrle, said the sheep was brought to his house on 24th of December. He examined it to see whether it had been skinned and cut by a practical butcher, and he at once said that it had not, the skin having the appearance of having been torn off. Mr Roper appeared for the prisoner, and asked whether it was not a fact that there was sufficient meat for domestic purposes in the house when they searched it, and he replied that there was, but that a raffle was to take place in the house, at which pieces of meat were offered as prizes. The prisoner was committed to the Assizes. Mr Bankes, reluctantly consented to bail, £40 and two sureties of £20 each.

Unfortunately we were unable to find out what happened to Mr Millington.

Murder at Model Farm

Model Farm is situated on Lower Mountain Road, Penyffordd, and had been bought by farmer Mr John J. Rowlands in 1921. He was vice-president of the Hawarden branch of the Farmer's Union, a member of the Rural District Council, the Board of Guardians and Treasurer of the Primitive Chapel Penyffordd. He had a wife and six children.

This murder hit the headlines in many local newspapers such as the *County Herald*, 13 March 1925. Mr Rowlands had apparently been shot dead by a poacher on March 5. Mr Rowlands had been out ferreting on the farm, as there were many rabbits, when he was told about a suspected poacher on his land. One of his wagoners, a Mr Joseph Evans, saw him go across the fields to challenge the man, and then saw the man behaving in a strange manner:

The County Herald gave a graphic report of events and continues at a later date with the trial, again we thought you might prefer to read the report, as it is so descriptive.

THE MURDER NEAR MOLD

Shortly before 6 o'clock on Thursday night, Mr John Rowlands, farmer of the Model Farm, Penyffordd near Mold, was shot dead by a man supposed to be a poacher, who made his escape, in a field adjoining his farm.

It is stated that Mr Rowlands had been out ferreting on his land, which contains many rabbits One of Mr Rowland's wagoners, named Evans, saw Mr Rowlands go back to the man, with whom he had previously spoken, evidently because the man had said something to him. The wagoner then saw Mr Rowlands and the man struggling, and in the struggle Rowlands fell to the ground. The man ran away.

When Mr Rowlands was picked up he was found to have been shot in three places, and when carried to the farmhouse he was dead.

The police description of the wanted man is: Height 5 ft 10 in; dark complexion, black moustache; dressed in a long coat, wearing knee breeches, and a soft cap or felt hat; and was carrying a gun.

The man was last seen going in the direction of Hope.

All night the search for the man was continued, in which more than 200 people took part, and all the next day and on to Saturday night, when Chief Inspector Cornish and Detective Sergeant Mallett, of Scotland Yard arrived and took charge of the investigations, They continued to search through Sunday.

Joseph Evans told a Press representative that he informed Mr Rowlands on Thursday that he had seen a strange man with a gun in one of the fields. Mr Rowlands went to speak to the man and according to Evans there was a struggle.

Evans states that three shots followed and Mr Rowlands collapsed. Evans ran to him, and he died in his arms.

Meanwhile the stranger made off after flourishing his gun in Evans's face.

The Inquest followed with the Flintshire Coroner Mr F. Llewelyn Jones, and was adjourned to 17 March. Once the culprit was caught he was committed for trial at the Flintshire Assizes on 5 March. The murder trial was reported on in the *Mold /Deeside/ Buckley Leader*, 19 June 1925, as follows:

THE MURDER TRIAL

The Assize Court has been crowded out during the hearing of the Penyffordd murder trial, and it has been difficult to get a seat anywhere in the court. Every inch of the public portion was taken up at the opening of the doors of the court after each adjournment a crowd flooded in and a rush was like a tap, and women were always in the forefront of the crowd. The small court soon became oppressive and about half a dozen people fainted the first day, and were carried out. At the dinner hour a lot of spectators did not go to their homes, but bringing out their lunch had something to eat on the County Hall field and were early waiting by the court door for it to re-open again. During the proceedings on Wednesday the judge warned the crowd that the court would be cleared if they laughed again. As the accused walked in and out of the dock the crowd strained themselves to get a glimpse of him, while each evening a morbid crowd assembled about the precincts of the railway station to see him being removed to the station for Walton Gaol, in charge of warders and police. On Wednesday the crowd was swelled by the presence of farmers and country people, who arriving a bit late, tried to jostle their way into court but failed. The result was there was always a large crowd outside the court, so an enterprising quack doctor moved his wares off the High Street and took up position on the roadway outside the court and carried on, but was eventually stopped because his voice was disturbing the court. The jury contained three local jurors, and once empanelled on Wednesday morning they were shepherded together and not allowed to go home. They were under the charge of a policeman and a governess, had their lunch brought to them during the day, and at the rising of the court were taken to the Black Lion Hotel, which was their quarters until they delivered their verdict. They have been out for motor rides and walks, but always under the eye of the law. A murder trial can be rendered invalid if an outside person speaks to a juror. Brennan, who took little interest in the trial, sitting on a chair in the dock practically motionless while it lasted, heard the verdict of the jury unconcerned. He was immediately taken away by warders, and as he walked to his cell brushed his forehead with his hand as though to wipe the perspiration. He was later taken to Walton Prison, Liverpool.

The accused poacher William Theodore Brennan aged 26 of Guildsborough House, Wrexham Road, Penyffordd, after a short trial was found guilty but insane. He was sent to Broadmoor Criminal Lunatic Asylum where he died some years later.

Primary and Secondary Sources

Introduction
FRO D/G/2690, Robronet, 1330.
FRO DM/126, Rhos y Brooner, 1737.
FRO B 561, Ryt y Devet, 1353.
FRO B 562, Stryt Isaf, 1362.
FRO D/M/134.
Place names of East Flintshire. H. W. Owen. (Univ. of Wales Press, 1994).

Part One

Flintshire. The distant past — A History for Schools, vol 1, C. R. Williams (Gee, 1961).
North Wales in the making. Michael Senior (Gwsag Carreg Gwalch, 1995).
Clwyd Magazine for North Wales, 1st Issue.
Growth and Development of Settlement Population in Flintshire, 1851-91, K. Davies, MSc.
The Archeology of Clwyd, David Hill.
Royal Commission of Ancient Monuments in Wales and Monmouthshire — Inventory of County of Flint, (pub. HMSO, 1912).
Thesis 'Wat's Dyke', Margaret Worthington.
Wat's Dyke a Field Survey, Cyril Fox.
Place names of East Flintshire, H. W. Owen (Univ. of Wales Press, 1994).

The Normans, 1066–1087
North Wales in the Making, Michael Senior (Gwsag Carreg Gwalch, 1995)
Flintshire (the dominance of the Norman Earl of Chester) J. M. Edwards, MA (Oxon), 1914.
Visitors guide to the Welsh Borders, Lawrence Garner. (Moorland, 1984)
Cheshire under the Norman Earls 1066-1237, B. M. C. Husain, vol.4, (Cheshire Community Council, 1973)
Flintshire from the Earliest Times, a History for Schools, vol. 1, C. R. Williams (Gee, 1961)
Britannica.com. website.
Pattern of Settlement, by G. R. Jones.
Domesday Cheshire.

The Welsh Princes/Rebellion
Life in Wales, A. H. Dodd (Batsford, 1972).
A History of Modern Wales, David Williams (John Murray).
Wales in the Early Middle Ages, Wendy Davies (Leicester Univ. Press, 1982.).
A History of Wales, John Davies (Allen Lane Penguin Press, 1993).
Wales Through the Ages, vol 1., A. J. Roderick. (C. Davies, Swansea, 1975).
Wales before 1536, Donald Gregory (Gwsag Carreg Gwalch, 1993).

The Civil War 1642–46
FRO D/DM/1411/41, Sequestered land from the Earl of Derby.
A Nation under Siege, the Civil War in Wales, 1642-48, Peter Gaunt (Cadw, 1991).
North Wales in the Civil War, Norman Tucker (Gwsag Gee, 1958).

Part Two

Enclosures
FRO D/DM/1411/36, Letter re trial 8. 4. 1794.
FRO D/LA/11/12, Hope Enclosure Act Hope Manor. 1791.
FRO D/LE/686, Letter re trial 31. 3. 1794.
CRO, Eaton Hall Estate Papers, 58.
FRO D/DM/268 2, Local Act for enclosure of land Pentrobin and Bannel 1798.
FRO QS/DE/10, Hope Enclosure Act plan and award 1797-98.
FRO QS/DE/7, Map ref. Enclosure Penyffordd.
Hope Marriage Register, 1780–1804.
Leeswood Hall Estate Papers.
Chester Chronicle, 29 July 1791.
'The House of Stanley', Peter Draper of Ormskirk, 1864.
History of the Old Parish of Hawarden, T. W. Pritchard (Bridge Books, 2002).

Agriculture
FRO D/LE/591, Labourers wages.
FRO D/DM/850/3, Hope Parish Poor Rate book.
FRO, Earl of Derby Box 8 G 1345.
19/323, box 8 /1-4.
The Forging of a Modern State, Eric J. Evans, 1783-1870 (2nd Edition, Longman, 1996).
Industrial Conflict 1870-1914, Clive Emsley (Open University).

Industry
FRO D/DM/190/19, Oil works in Leeswood area.
FRO D/DM/434/99, Oil Shale and Cannel Coal, Institute of Petroleum, 1938, H. P. Griffard.
FRO Census Returns, 1841/51/61/71/81/91/1901.
O/S/Map, 1871, 25 inches to 1 mile.
FRO D/DM/345/1, Flint Electoral Roll.
Mineral Statistics Report, 1865.
Flintshire Historical Society Publication, vol. 25, p.166–9, 'The Distillation of Oil from Cannel Coal', H. H. Gregory.
Industry in Clwyd, C. J. Williams (Clwyd Record Office, 1986).
Industrial Revolution in North Wales, A. H. Dodd (Univ. of Wales Press, 1951).
Slater's Trade Directory, 1860/70.

Travel/Transport/ Communication
FRO L 907-2.
FRO QS/DT/15, 1834 Road from Abermorddu to Lower King's Ferry.
FRO QS/DT/3, 1821 Road Mold to Broughton.
FRO QS/MB, Quarter sessions minute book.
FRO QS/DT/3R, 1821 Hawarden road.
Hidden Highways of North Wales, R. J. Dutton (Redwood Books, 1997).
The Roads of North Wales, 1750–1850, A. H. Dodd.
Flintshire History Society, Book 21, 'Turnpike Roads'.
From Family History to Community History, Volume 2, edited by W. T. R. Pryce (Cambridge Univ. Press, OU).
Wrexham Mold & Connah's Quay Railway, by J. M. Dunn (Oakwood Press, 1957).
The Denbigh and Mold Line, W. G. Rear (Foxline Publishing).

The Rebecca Riots
FRO 93/84, records reader.
Rioting in North Wales 1536–1918, Tim Jones (Bridge Books, 1997).
Mid Victorian Britain 1851–75 Geoffrey Best (Fontana Press, 1990).

Education
Education Act, 1870.
Penyffordd School.
FRO E/X/48/1, Record of cases of Corporal Punishment, 1910.
FRO E/SB/2/8, Account Ledger for Hope School Board.
FRO E/SB/2/3, Contract to build Penyffordd School.
FRO E/AR/48/1, Penyffordd school Admission Register, 1875–1916.
FRO E/LB/48/1 & 2, Penyffordd Village school Log Books, 1875–1896 & 1896–1930.
FRO FC/E/8/79, correspondence, 1928–1962.
FRO FC/A/2/21, Plan for Penyffordd School, 1923.
FRO D/DM/4/2/2, Music Certificate.
FRO FC/E/8/79, Inspectors report, 1941–1950.
FRO E/LB/48/2, Inspectors reports, 1896, 1904, 1909, 1916, 1940.
Leaflet on the history of school. R. L. Parry.
Newspaper cuttings.
Penymynydd school Log Books, 1886–1894, 1894–1950, 1950–1959.
Minute Book, 1904–1960.
FRO FC/E/8/78, Inspectors report.
FRO D/MA/1659, Proposed alterations early 20th century.
FRO P/28/1/195, Plans to install water carriage system 1958.
FRO P/28/1/196, Plans for indoor pupils' toilets.
Plans for first floor extensions late 1970s.
FRO FC/E/8/78, Pentrobin correspondence.
FRO E/X/13, Minute book vol 1. Deed Poll 1852, Land conveyance.
FRO D/DM/1213/B/1/3, Closure of Pentrobin school 1964.
Royal Commission on Elementary Education in Wales, 1847.
The History of Parish of Hawarden, vol. 2, W. Bell Jones, 1945 (unpublished MS).
St. John's the Baptist Voluntary Aided Primary School Prospectus, 2003.

The Churches of Penyffordd and Penymynydd
FRO D/TR/312, Letter re building of Methodist Chapel, Stryt Issa.
FRO D/DM/434/72, Notes on chapel by C. Duckworth.
N/31/19, Notes on Penyffordd Methodist Chapel.
FRO D/BJ/197.
FRO D/BJ/130, 216.
Notes from Charles Duckworth.
Mount Tabor booklet compiled by J. Malcom Brown and Lesley Piercy.
History of Hope, A. R. Maddocks.
Zion Presbyterian Church Penyffordd, a short history, 1840–1990.
Emmanuel Church Penyffordd, 1993 and its history.

Meadowslea Hospital
CRO, Central Cheshire at the opening of the 20th century — contemporary biographies, W. T. Pike & Co.
CR/60/3/34, The Frosts and Meadows 1641–1874, Thomas Hughes.
FRO D/CE/1/3.
FRO NT/1152, Memorial to the King.

FRO D/DM/130/10.
FRO E/55/4/84, information about the hospital.
FRO E/55/4/85, information about the hospital.
Health Authority Archives, Mold.

Part Three

Shops /Inns/ Houses
FRO D/DM/2, Sale notice for Duke of Wellington.
FRO FC/C/4/2/8, Detailed return of fully licensed house and beer house Mold 1892.
FRO F/P/52, Return of fully licensed house and off license 1903.
FRO D/DM/662/30, Agreement between J. Thomas Crown Inn and John Fox Castle Hill Brewery Ewloe.
FRO NT/1546, List of premises supplied by Northgate Brewery.
FRO D/BC/3306, Correspondence re- sale Horse and Jockey 1879.
FRO G/A/164/1, Inspection of Rhyd y Defaid Rural Sanitary Authority.
FRO B/561, Ryt-y-Devet.
Sale agreement between Ward & Peters 30th Nov. 1868 (private papers owned by Mr Ivor Edwards).
DBL 13015, 1998.
FRO Box 8 38/848, Sale of properties 15th June 1848 sold by Edward Bartley's Executors.
FRO P/31/1/24-25, 1850 Tithe Map and apportionments.
FRO LB/482, Penyffordd school log book 2.
FRO NT/1650, Life of Frank Hurlbutt 1866–1944.
FRO D/DM/1195/7, Advertisements.
Census Returns, 1841/61/71/81/91/1901.
FRO D/BC/3314, Sale agreement between Vaughan and Sievewright 1931.
Slater's Trade Directory for North Wales, 1883, 1868, 1885, 1895.
Cassey's Trade Directory, 1876.
Bennett's Business Directory, 1913, 1914, 1936.
Cope Directory, 1932.
Advertisement from booklet on St John's Church Penymynydd, 1939.
Advertisements from Fête Programme 1955.
Annual Report of the County Archivist.
Castle Hill Brewery, by P. F. Mason, 1979.
Information from Flintshire Planning & Development Dept. Listed buildings and detail.
Ian Williams, former owner The Rhyd.
Newspaper cuttings, July 1908 (Howell Hughes).
Hope Parish Magazine no.6. Jan. 981 Hurlbutt family.
Then and Now Village History. Penyffordd, Penymynydd and Dobshill Women's Institute. (Castell Alun High School).

Utilities
Memorial Institute minutes.
FRO D/DM/400/7, Water rates 1927.
FRO G/A/164/1.
FRO D/DM/661/6, Nuisance and Abatement /Sanitary.
FRO D/DM/1277/1, Pest Control.
Mrs Lilian Hewitt.

Sport/Entertainment/Organisations
FRO D/DM/785/4, Musical Entertainment.

FRO D/JB/148, War time information leaflets.
Tennis Club minute book, 1949–71.
Western Advertiser.
Wrexham Leader.
Chester Chronicle.
Hope Parish Magazine.
Village Voices, ed. P. Dudgeon (W. F. Books, 1990).

War
FRO D/JB/96, Feeding and shelter, food from Red Cross/ Stirrup Pump.
FRO, *Clwyd at War 1939–45.*
FRO D/DM/1277/1, Women's Land Army Flintshire WW2.
FRO FC/E/8/78.
Hope Parish Magazines.
Chester Chronicle cuttings, Mr Howell Hughes.
A Dictionary of Military Uniform, W. Y. Carman (Book Club Associates).
'Luftwaffe over Clwyd', Ivor Wynne Jones, *Transactions of the Denbighshire Historical Society.*
Wartime Buckley, Philip Edwards.
Information from the Regimental Museum of the Royal Welch Fusiliers, Lt. Col. P. A. Crocker (Rtd.).
Mr A. Astbury, MBE.
Mr Cyril Edwards.

The War Memorial Institute
FRO D/CL/185, Programme of competative meeting, 1932.
FRO D/DM/1195/1, Poster for public meeting.
FRO D/DM/1195/7, Fête Programme, 1955.
FRO D/DM/1195/9, Minute book for Institute, 1923.
FRO D/DM/1195/10, Minute book, 1930.
Newspaper cuttings, various.
Hope Parish Magazine, December 1918.
Wrexham Leader, 21July 1923.
Flintshire Observer, July 1923.
Chester Chronicle, 26 July 1923.

Crime and mystery
MF 249, *County Herald,* 13 and 20 March, 1925.
MF 280, *Mold/Deeside/Buckley Leader,* 19 June, 1925.
The Penyffordd Poacher, by Steve Fielding.
FRO D/DM/410/1, the Kinnerton Sheep Stealer.
Mr Ivor Edwards.
Buckley Magazine, No. 17, Derrick Pratt.
Gordon Hill, MSc.
Mr Steve Grenter, Wrexham Museum.